PLAYING
for KEEPS

*Dating, Seducing,
& (maybe) Marrying
the Modern Man*

JUDY COLE

Adams Media Corporation
Holbrook, Massachusetts

Published by
Adams Media Corporation
260 Center Street, Holbrook, MA 02343

ISBN: 1-55850-766-3

 PRINTED IN CANADA

J I H G F E D C B A

Library of Congress Cataloging-in-Publication Data
Cole, Judy.
Playing for keeps : dating, securing & (maybe) marrying the modern man /
Judy Cole.
          p.   cm.
          ISBN 1-55850-766-3 (pbk.)
1. Dating (Social customs) 2. Man-woman relationships. 3. Women—Psychology.
4. Women—Sexual behavior. 5. Self-esteem in women. I. Title
                    HQ801.C65   1997
          646.7'7—dc21   97–25530
                                    CIP

This book is available at quantity discounts for bulk purchases.
For information, call 1-800-872-5627 (in Massachusetts, 617-767-8100).

Visit our home page at http://www.adamsmedia.com

Contents

To my parents, Earl and Natalie, who didn't make as many mistakes as they would like to believe; to Beth, who helped me get my foot in the door; and Anne, who let me keep it there.

Thanks.

Introduction

IF YOU WERE LUCKY enough to grow up knowing your grandmother—or watching *The Waltons*—you were probably treated to a healthy helping of homespun hints regarding the best techniques for concocting light and flaky piecrusts, baking perfect loaves of bread, hemming skirts, removing mayonnaise stains from silk blouses, and so on. And what more important advice could that generation of venerated ladies pass on to our eager ears than how to get—and keep—the man of our dreams? After all, to steer courageously and correctly through the teeming sea of prospective suitors who would someday be clambering after us with proposals (of marriage, that is), we needed a rudder. And damn it, our grannies had already navigated those waters and come home with the golden fleece—or, in my grandmother's case, an insurance salesman.

Since my Gram Clara and Grampa Max had been married for fiftysomething years (yikes!) by the time I was a teenager, she must be doing something right, I reasoned. So what if he turned off his hearing aid every time she came into the room, when not ten seconds before he'd been glued to the play-by-play of the Illinois/Notre Dame game that had been wafting in faintly through the open window courtesy of his next-door neighbor's radio—and cursing vigorously under his breath every time the Illini fumbled the ball deep in their own territory. So what if every piece of furniture they owned was shrink-wrapped to asphyxiation in clear, unforgiving plastic that always stuck to you, leading to that awful moment when you tried to extricate yourself from its unintentionally juicy embrace and it emitted an ungodly "thwuck," leaving an ostentatious scarlet hickey on the exposed flesh of your thigh? They were happy, weren't they?

They had the house, two handsome, thriving sons, and Pal, the wonder dog. A new Oldsmobile appeared in their driveway like clockwork every three years to replace the old model. They played bridge socially; he golfed, she belonged to a mah-jongg club. They had the life. And if I knew what was good for me, I could get the life, too—provided I was willing to play by the time-honored rules for winning the heart of Mr. Right. And who better to show me the choreography of that particular mating dance than one who had walked the walk (down the aisle) and talked the talk ("I do")? In short, my grandmother.

When I was about sixteen, Clara, sensing that I was on the brink of womanhood, decided it was time to indoctrinate me in the fine traditions of man-catching. No matter that, to the best of my recollection, I was something of a late bloomer, caring for boys only in the most abstract romantic sense. She was determined to start me off on the right foot, so one fine day, she sat me down, fixed her searching brown eyes on me with a level gaze that was both knowing and sincere, and gave me the following brief but pithy advice: "Judy," she said, "if you want to get a man, you must never smoke cigars." Frankly, this wasn't exactly the earth-shattering epiphany I was expecting. The confusion that registered on my bewildered face induced her to continue. "No man will ever marry a girl who smokes cigars," she declared. "They make your breath bad and turn your teeth yellow."

"I see," I said, even though I wasn't sure I did. "Thanks, Gram." Was I to take this to mean that my future would be assured as long as I steered away from stogies? Would any mate my heart desired be mine for the asking, as long as I forsook the cheroot? Could it be possible that a great, sunny harvest of marvelous men would spread out like an orchard before me, each prince more charming, smart, bright, witty, and rich than the one before, as long as I never lit up? What if the temptation became too much? If I ever had a hankering for a Havana, I supposed I could always sneak out behind the garage to satisfy my illicit cravings, once I'd copped the requisite jewelry, but wouldn't that be cheating? (Aw, but on the other hand, who would know?)

Her next advice? "You should start wearing a girdle. Men aren't interested in girls who look sloppy." It seemed, to my grandmother's way of thinking, that any woman who went out in public without proper corseting was committing an act against fashion tantamount to treason. "And get your hair cut," she threw in for good measure.

Wait a minute. This was dangerously simple. While the girdle and the haircut gave me pause, the cigar thing would be a piece of cake. There had to be more to bagging a prize husband than this—and, of course, there was. For these particular pearls of my grandmother's wisdom, to mix metaphors, were only the tip of the iceberg. There was an endless, dizzying array of rules, regs, and dos and don'ts that my grandmother assured me were requisite to winning and keeping my man—all of that "one step forward, two steps back" kind of stuff, the nodding-your-head-and-smiling-politely-while-you're-

bored-out-of-your-head gambit. These rules seemed justi-
fiable if you were trapped in the company of your maid-
en aunts for an hour, but appalling in the context of a
woman-to-man relationship.

You were never to let on to a potential admirer that
you entertained anything more than a casual interest in
him — especially if you did. The more a man wanted you,
the more aloof you were expected to be. You could be
perceived as charming, attentive, even concerned — but
not *interested*. You were never to call a man up or appear
too available. "Men must do the chasing," my grandmother insisted. "Of course they'll *take* a woman who
falls into their laps," she intoned with knowing innuendo, "but they won't *keep* her. You must maintain your distance at all times — until the proposal."

"But won't the man just get fed up, go off, and find
someone else who isn't so difficult?" I wanted to know.

"Ah," said my grandmother, "there's an art to this
kind of negotiation. You have to learn how to seem
encouraging without appearing *easy*. You must give your
suitors the impression that they are on the verge of catching you, but when they get too close, you must always
put yourself just a little further out of reach."

"So you can never tell a man you'd like to date him?"
I asked incredulously.

"Certainly not!" Clara retorted with the exasperated
tone she always used to imply that my mother hadn't
exactly raised me right.

Just who did you have to be to win the man of your
dreams — a Stepford Wife? And just what kind of marriage were you likely to have if you played by the rules?

As I said, my grandparents were together for over
fifty years, and they always made a great fuss about the
fact that they loved each other, but as I grew older, I
began to have a sneaking suspicion that if you scratched

the shiny veneer, something darker would turn up. And I was right.

It may have been true that my grandfather put my grandmother on a pedestal and that Gram accepted him as king of their castle, but it's my guess that neither one ever really knew what the other was about (or if they did, they never let on). My grandmother spent her life keeping up appearances, being who she was *supposed to be*, rather than *who she was*, and my grandfather did pretty much the same. Still, on the surface things were status quo, ducks in a row, apple-pie order — albeit slipcovered in Saran Wrap.

Eventually, it dawned on me that "having it all" might not be everything it was cracked up to be. I thought of the occupational hazards of living life on a pedestal — the nosebleeds from being far above reality, the frozen expression from keeping that stiff upper lip, the headaches from staring unflinchingly toward the horizon as life went on around me, that broomstick I'd have to store where the sun doesn't shine to maintain my perfect posture, not to mention that symbolic girdle that one never left the house without — which, I now understood, was designed to rein in a lot more than just my wayward tummy. None of these things held the slightest appeal.

What did I do? Like any normal teenager, I rebelled, of course. There was someone out there who was going to love me for me, not for how well I played the games fixed by a society that I judged to be outdated and extinct, but for the person I was inside, what I thought and felt — and I never doubted for an instant that destiny would bring us together.

Standing steadfast on my soapbox, filled with the burning, self-righteous ideals that can only be powered by the stubbornness of youth, I resolved to make my own rules and come up with my own answers. I was convinced that men and women could overcome the differences of gender and be people first. I launched myself on a personal quest to find a Mr. Right who marched to the beat of my newfound drummer, and with him, to create a paradise on earth. *Blast sexual stereotypes,* I caviled. *Full speed ahead!* (In short, I became really, really annoying.)

Like Dorothy in *The Wizard of Oz*, I went down the whole length of the yellow brick road in order to discover that the truth had been staring me in the face all along. I *can* have it all, but only I can define what "all" is *for me.* And the same goes for you.

If history is here for anything, it's here as a teacher. Sure, the world is a different place than it was sixty, seventy — even ten years ago, and it's hard to keep up with what "having it all" really means, since "it" changes every fifteen minutes. However, some things haven't really changed. Eventually, I came back around the other side of the circle and realized that Gram may not have been 100 percent right, but she wasn't 100 percent wrong, either.

It's safe to say that nowadays, I look back on Gram's advice about the art of man-catching and take it all with more than a few grains of salt. Still, it can't be denied that men do love the chase. Since most men in our society are conditioned to be achievement-oriented, they want to think that when it comes to dating, they're catching a prize. But that doesn't necessarily mean they want to bring home a woman who is a doormat — or a princess. Sure, there are men out there who need to let their egos and sense of entitlement rule their actions, but a good man wants a life partner who can think for herself, has her own opinions, and can be his equal.

And don't be fooled into thinking that men have cornered the market on the "easy come, easy go" syndrome. We women are just as guilty of rejecting potential suitors who do not challenge us. If we look back in our pasts, most of us have at least one "Gee, you're a real nice guy, but let's just be friends" skeleton in our romantic closet. You know who I'm talking about—that guy who wanted you so, so badly and would probably have treated you like gold, but was about as appealing as day-old oatmeal when it came to being an object of your affections.

Ironically, while reflecting on all of the wisdom that my grandmother tried to impart to me and sifting through her extensive catalogue of how-tos, I came across another lesson that may have been (however unintentionally) the most valuable one she passed along. The most indispensable thing my grandmother taught me? How to make a perfect piecrust. Yup, a piecrust.

Great romance is like great pastry. The basic ingredients don't vary all that much, and while some may prefer butter to shortening, the most important factor for achieving optimum results is knowing how to adjust your ingredients to the prevailing conditions of the day. Is the climate hot or cold? Dry or humid? Can the temperature in your oven be trusted, or does it have to be checked for accuracy? No one set of rules can be right for every occasion, nor for every man or romantic relationship.

In life, love, and piecrust, you have to allow for flux and variation. It's the only way you can be assured of your just desserts. How do I know? Let's just say that when it comes to romance, I've made and eaten a lot of piecrusts. Not all of them were perfect, and some were downright disasters, but I've also had my fair share of delightful treats as well. And you can have yours too.

Men and women *are* truly different, and there are some things inherent to our natures that must be taken into account. But there's no reason to put aside being who you are for the sake of love. All you need is to like yourself, trust yourself, be willing to be loved for who and what you are—and use some common sense.

And who knows? Maybe you don't even want pie, or marriage. Perhaps you're a strudel gal who's looking for a long-term love without live-in implications, or maybe you'd rather just grab a cookie as you're running out the door. Whatever your particular hunger, there's a world of possibility waiting to satisfy it. If you keep an open mind and don't let yourself get sucked in by the climate of paranoia being peddled by the savvy spin doctors looking to cash in on the female angst of the hour, you'll do just fine.

Anyone who has turned on a TV, scanned a newspaper, or picked up a magazine lately is more than likely familiar with "backlash" — the boogie-man currently being raised to undermine women's sense of autonomy, especially in matters of love. Some of the advocates of backlash are raking in big money by telling us it's time to go back to the future. These folks know how to push all the right buttons. They hit us where we live by putting a name on one of our biggest terrors. "The new way isn't working," they warn. "And if you don't hop onto our bandwagon, you're going to spend your life alone." No doubt about it, it's powerful stuff.

As a result of buying into this particular party line, many women today are running the risk of seriously shortchanging their own best interests. Convinced that if they act honestly they're going to wind up as crazy old spinsters with an abundance of cats and no husband, they are turning back the clock to a time when women had few choices and were expected to live a domesticated lifestyle. Let's differentiate between *domestic* and *domesticated* here. I got a grade of 98 in Home Economics, I cook, and I sew. I'm a whiz with crafts — not to mention light plumbing and wallpapering. But I'm not tame — and I'm not apologizing.

Sure, you can buy into the fear that you'll never find a man if you express what you really think as a woman. But ask yourself, "Do I really want to? Do I really have to play games to get and keep a man's affections?"

I'm not suggesting that you should expect love to just fall into your lap or come knocking at your door. Everyone knows the world is a lot more complex than it was when our grandmothers were in their courting days. I have no desire to go back to the 1920s to find my soul mate. He's not back there. And I'm betting that if you're a woman who can hold down a job, run a household — the whole nine yards — yours isn't either. You absolutely do not have to get on that bus! But, of course, if you truly believe that the good old way will lead you to the kind of life that appeals, have we got a book for you — but not this one.

The Total You

CHAPTER ONE

Make Yourself Over in Your Own Best Image

IF YOU'RE ALREADY SATISFIED with your counterpart on the other side of the looking glass, congratulations. You're one of the lucky ones, and you can skip over Part One and go right to Part Two. However, most women are raised to believe that other people's tastes and values are more important than their own. Thus, it can become difficult for us to separate what we truly want from the things that have over the course of time been imposed on us from the outside.

The first step toward having a healthy, fun, fulfilling relationship with a lover is to have a healthy, fun, fulfilling relationship with yourself. How can you accomplish this? Give yourself an honest evaluation, and don't fall into the trap of allowing bad habits to rule your life because you've talked yourself into believing that they are "the real you." To get to the heart of you, you're going to have to plow through every opinion you have about yourself and weed out the ones that aren't really yours. You're going to have to shine a light in every dark corner of your personality, reexamine the choices you make on a day-to-day basis, and see if they truly suit you.

A good way to start is to size up your assets and your liabilities and examine ways in which you can accentuate your good points. Next, learn to recognize areas in your life that need work. Then, give yourself permission to make yourself over in your own best image. Bear in mind that even the most contented, self-realized people have at least one or two personal issues they'd like to tinker with. So, no matter whether you're looking at a minor adjustment or a major overhaul, there are a few things you should focus on before you begin:

1. **Do this for you.** Believe it or not, the only opinion that truly counts about you is your own. No one can make peace with yourself but you. You can reinvent your image to try to fit in wherever you go and never really be who you are, or you can trust and believe in yourself and be comfortable anywhere you go.

2. **Be honest with yourself, but don't beat yourself up.** This isn't an exercise in masochism. If there's something about yourself that you feel needs fixing — either internally or externally — it doesn't mean that you're a failure. Every human being is a work in progress. Whatever needs tinkering with is more than likely just something you haven't figured out yet, or haven't been willing to face. But take a lesson from the greatest artists of history. Even masters like Rembrandt and Picasso went back to the easel time after time until the picture on the canvas realized the image in their minds. You don't have to get it right the first try, or even the second or third. And remember, mistakes are not tragedies, they're tools for learning. Even if you screw up, it isn't etched in stone.

3. **Being self-aware is not the same as being selfish.** You deserve to have what you want in life. We all do. This does not mean we should treat others badly. It doesn't mean we should berate little old ladies who have fifteen items in the ten-item line at the supermarket, or

that we should launch a nuclear missile at someone who accidentally bumps into us on the subway. It does mean that we should know our own boundaries and comfort zones and not violate them to please others. You don't have to be a dishrag for men to like you. Sure, men like to be pampered, but in the long run, the ones who are only interested in dating or marrying someone they can control and manipulate aren't worth being with in the first place.

4. **Being different isn't wrong.** We all tend to concentrate on the outer stuff: "My rear end looks like a Mack truck." "I'm too flat-chested." "My teeth are crooked." "You could land a DC-10 on my nose." We've all got flaws. Well, not flaws really—deviations from the accepted standards of beauty. And you know what? So what! Okay, if you've got a physical attribute that truly makes your life miserable, then go ahead and change it if you think it will make you feel better—but before you go under the knife, make sure the only person you are out to please is yourself. If you give up the things that go into making you unique, you run the risk of winding up being like everybody else.

5. **You don't have to do everything all at once.** If you have a lot of things you want to work on, just pick one to start with. Don't think of things in terms of a huge project that you can never finish. Think of it as a process that you can take one step at a time.

6. **You don't have to change overnight.** If you've got a lifetime of programming to examine and rewire, don't expect to just go to bed one night determined to change and wake up a new you the next morning. Old habits die hard, and old beliefs are the same.

7. **You can't make a real soufflé out of powdered eggs.** This is one bit of Grandma's advice that holds true. Yes, you can reinvent yourself in almost any way you'd

like, but keep your expectations within the realm of reality. If you're five-two and big-boned, no matter how pretty you may be, chances are that you're never going to be a Paris runway model. That doesn't mean you can't be beautiful, wear great clothes, and have men falling all over you. Find your own personal style and let it flourish; that should do the trick.

8. **Life isn't always fair.** Feeling right with yourself does not guarantee that Prince Charming will ride up and sweep you off your feet: Nothing that I or anyone else can tell you will work every time.

A helpful approach to finding the road to the best possible you is to look at the task as a role-playing game where you get to be both a reporter and the person being interviewed. Your goal is to get to know yourself, realize your strengths and weaknesses, and within realistic expectations become the you that you'd most like to be. Explore what you like best about yourself and figure out ways to let those assets shine.

Begin with the inner you and work your way out. Clothes, hair, and makeup are important, and by all means, get to them, but they should be the last items on this agenda. The first thing you'll need to do is ask yourself some serious questions and be as truthful as you can about the answers.

A good journalist knows that to get to the real story, you can't just ask about the "what" — you've got to delve into the who, how, when, and why of it all. Things get to be the way they are for specific reasons. You're going to have to be your own detective and go back and uncover, layer by layer, the course of events that made you who you are today. This isn't about blame, it's about understanding and acceptance.

Taking Stock of the Inner You

The way in which we perceive and value both our faults and virtues can speak volumes about our self-esteem. For this exercise, let's start with the good.

1. Choose your best asset — the one characteristic in your life that most pleases you.

It could be that you're very savvy when it comes to making business decisions. Perhaps you're a born problem solver. Maybe your greatest happiness in life comes from being able to help other people, or possibly you've got an artistic talent like music, poetry, or painting that you love to express. It might be something as simple as being very honest. Maybe you're someone who is willing to take chances, or you're of that special breed that has the stick-to-it-iveness to always see things through to the end. (If you've chosen something about yourself that's on a purely physical level — like "I've got a great figure, eyes, smile (fill in the blank) — then you're not delving deep enough.)

Think of an incident in your life when your particular personal plus came into play in a positive way. Can you begin to see why this attribute is your best feature, and what there is about it that makes it important to you?

Now take a closer look and ask yourself, *If no one else ever knew about this trait, would I still derive pleasure from it?* Often, we pursue things and behave in certain ways not because they are truly pleasing to us, but for the attention we can derive from them. Says Selina, "I was always the classic do-gooder. I volunteered for everything, signed up for a hundred committees, was a brave little soldier for whatever cause I'd joined that week. I didn't question authority, I just went along, thinking that if I gave and

gave and gave, it would automatically bring me acceptance and love—but I was wrong.

"One day, I came to the realization that by spreading
my efforts so thin, I wasn't doing anyone any good—
least of all myself. It was at that point that I learned to say
no and to pull back. To my shock, the world didn't end.
Sure, some feathers got ruffled when I finally stood up
for myself, but I had to stop trying to be everything to
everybody and focus on what mattered to me for a
change.

"These days, I still do volunteer work, but now, I
don't sit back and take orders, I give them. And you
know what? I'm damn good at it! I get a lot more accomplished than ever before, and on top of that, I feel a whole
lot better about myself at the end of the day."

If you have chosen something such as a talent, is it
something you truly derive satisfaction from or just
something that other people pat you on the back for? For
example, when Ellen was six, she found she had a talent
for playing the piano. Her mother was so thrilled she
immediately found a teacher for her and set up a rigorous
schedule of lessons and practice times. Ellen excelled at
her studies, but at the age of eight, she discovered baseball, and from that moment on, for her, the sun rose and
set on the playing field.

More than anything else in the world, she wanted to
play in Little League—but her mother couldn't understand this desire, and wrote it off as just a phase Ellen
was going through. She insisted that Ellen continue her
piano lessons and dreamed that someday her daughter
might play at Carnegie Hall. The choice for Ellen was a
fairly simple though unhappy one: Play the piano and
Mommy loves me. Play baseball and Mommy gets mad.
Being a "good" child, Ellen eventually capitulated, growing up to become a competent, if uninspired, pianist. She

continued to play as an adult whenever the occasion demanded, but while she craved the positive feedback her performances brought, the actual playing itself gave her no pleasure.

On the other hand, if there is something that gives you genuine satisfaction, do you pursue it wholeheartedly, or do you hold back for fear of being thought selfish? Practically from the time Sarah could hold a pencil, she was writing. Even at an early age, she had a keen wit and an eye for detail. At times, her constant scribblings nearly drove her parents to distraction. "One time," she reports, "my mom came in at about two in the morning and I was huddled under my blanket with a flashlight and a notebook working away furiously on a ghost story I was trying to finish. She almost blew a gasket. It was *way* past my bedtime. She grabbed the things away from me and told me I was to go to sleep that instant.

"But the next morning, instead of being mad, she just handed me back the notebook and said that in the future, I wasn't to stay up past ten o'clock. Then she smiled and gave me a big hug and told me how proud she was of me for finding something I was willing to work so hard for. It's funny, I didn't actually find out until many years later what she thought of my writing. And maybe that's a good thing, because it enabled me to write with my own voice, not one I thought others might want to hear."

Are there some other things you can think of that you'd like to try that you believe would give you similar satisfaction? If you haven't already tried them, what's stopping you? When you love yourself and love what you're doing, it not only gives your life meaning (as long as it doesn't consume your every waking moment), it makes you lovable to others as well. Examine the things that make you the happiest, celebrate them, and expand them whenever you can.

2. What's your least favorite thing about yourself?

Why does this particular thing displease you so much? Think back in time. Can you trace this negative aspect of your life to a specific incident or pattern of behavior? Was this thing something you were ever ridiculed for among your peers? Is it something that you feel others have and you lack?

Perhaps when you were in high school, you were not part of the "in" crowd—or any crowd for that matter. Maybe you felt like Isadora Duncan trapped in a herd of cheerleaders. Maybe you were one of those girls who learned to like boys at an early age and got a reputation for being "easy," or maybe you became known as one who wouldn't "put out" and got labeled a prude. Maybe you were a stick with "too much" ambition who knew her own mind and wound up stigmatized as a witch minus the w, plus a b.

Many of us count as our worst faults things that others are trying to make us feel bad about, or behavior that is a direct result of being made to feel left out when we were growing up. Of her high school experience, Renata recalls that everyone thought she was stuck-up. "It was so ridiculous! Here these guys were, putting me on this pedestal, and I could tell that they were thinking that *I* thought I was too good for them, when in reality I stayed home dateless and despairing on prom night because everyone assumed I'd already been asked. For the longest time, I couldn't figure out how to turn the situation around and let people know otherwise.

"I didn't want to be aloof, but since we'd moved around so much when I was a kid, I was afraid of letting anyone get too close to me. The last thing I wanted was to be an ice queen, but for the longest time, I just couldn't seem to help myself. The whole thing was so frustrating that there was many a night I cried myself to sleep.

"There's no point blaming the kids in school for not being able to understand — they just weren't old enough or broad enough to be able to comprehend what was going on. Hell, it took me a long time to figure it out myself! Once I did see what was going on, it still took time to change it, but if you want something badly enough, you can make it happen . . . and with some hard work and good breaks in the man department, eventually, I did."

Another account comes from Gloria, who used to think of herself as "too bright for her own good."

"When I was younger," she explains, "I had a need to be overly sarcastic. And while on the one hand, it bothered me, I couldn't seem to let a straight line go by without an overwhelming desire to pounce on it. When I'd meet a man, I'd practically torture him to death in an attempt to test his mental mettle.

"Because I considered myself 'smart,' I reasoned that any man worth my time had to be the same. But the result of this behavior was a lot of pissed-off people and unnecessary cruelty, because at the heart of it all, I was insecure about being perceived as anything other than a shining intellect. Coming from a family that on both sides had more than its fair share of brainiacs, I always harbored a secret fear that I wasn't going to measure up. It's a good thing I finally realized that no one in my family, or out of it, would love me any less if my IQ varied by a point or two, and once I figured that out, my need to act out this way evaporated."

So, when you decide to take a long, hard look at what you think your worst flaws may be, try to understand their underlying causes. Sometimes, shining a light on them has the same effect as throwing water on the Wicked Witch of the West — they just melt into a puddle and you're free to step over them and go on with your life.

3. Do you apologize all the time?

Do you find yourself bending over backward to accommodate people around you at the sacrifice of your own needs? Why do you think you do this?

If you find that you're constantly saying you're sorry and bending over backward to please those around you, this may be a signal that you do not value your own needs or trust your own ability to make decisions. Don't think that you're alone. Many, many women are brought up to believe that someone else—anyone else—is more qualified to make decisions about their lives than they are.

From Daddy, to boyfriend, to husband, women have traditionally been taught to hand over their autonomy to the men in their lives, and a lot of them feel that no one will love them if they don't. Don't get me wrong. There's nothing the matter with being kind, being a good friend, or even going out of your way for people, if that's your nature—but always doing for others without attending to your own needs doesn't make you a better person, it makes you less of one. This can be a hard pattern to change, but it's worth the effort. You don't have to go to the other extreme and be shrill or bitchy—just be clear and fair about the things you want, and don't be afraid to state your case. Everyone, including yourself, will like you better for it.

4. Do you avoid speaking your mind?

Do you say just the things you believe will gain you more social acceptance? Do you follow rather than lead for fear of not being liked? Do you pretend to be less intelligent than you are so men won't find you intimidating? Have you always been this way? What would you consider the worst possible outcome if you actually said or did the things you truly felt if they didn't fall into line with what others expected or desired from you?

Women are so often locked into their need to "fit in" that they allow peer pressure to steer them toward behavior that may not be in their best interests. We all want to be liked and loved, but being held in esteem for being something we're not is a lie. You have a brain. Use it. Make choices and take responsibility for the results. People who understand will support you; those who would think less of you for expressing yourself aren't worthy of your affection.

5. When you date, are you thinking only about marriage?

Do you believe that you can't be happy unless you've got a man in your life? There are women who truly believe that we were put on this earth to be part of a unit of two. There are some who feel that marriage, like air or water, is necessary to sustain life, and that their own existence is pointless without a partner. Then there are women who, after exploring all the options and carefully thinking them through, come to the conclusion that they would feel most happy and fulfilled pursuing a life that includes someone to share and build it with, but are self-realized enough to know that they aren't going to dry up and blow away if they haven't found that man yet, or they happen to be temporarily between partners. Next there are those who, after exploring all the options and carefully thinking them through, decide that they like themselves, that they are challenged and happy in their work, that they enjoy their friends, and that whether they are single or "coupled" has no real bearing on their overall state of well-being. And finally, there are those women who don't care to have any long-term partners at all, thank you.

Now, most of us fall into one of these categories, but if you answered "yes" to most of these questions, you should take a good, long look at how you came to hold these beliefs. Many women who choose this path as adults grew up in environments where negative female stereotypes were reinforced on a daily basis. If you were taught by word and deed that you could not be successful or even hope to take care of yourself without a man; if you were shown again and again that your opinions mattered less than the opinions of those around you; if you were put in a position that made it clear that in order to be considered acceptable by your family you would have to objectify yourself and sell yourself to whatever man would someday be responsible for you; then it's small wonder that you may have lost touch with the real "you."

If you grew up without positive role models to guide you, it's going to be tough to separate yourself from your upbringing — even if you do know what you want. Learning to assert yourself will take time and sometimes outside help. You will also meet resistance from members of your family and even some friends who are used to a "you" who doesn't rock the boat. People who expect certain behavior can become very bad-tempered and even downright mean when their expectations are challenged. What you're going to have to make them understand is that this isn't about blaming them, nor is it about abandoning them, but it is about you deciding what it's going to take to get you to a life that you can live with.

Once you've given yourself some time and space to think things through, you may find yourself feeling angry and betrayed. You may want to lash out or "get even" with those who have let you down. You also may find yourself hard pressed not to use your self-revelations as weapons and ammunition to hurt the people who raised you. If that is your inclination, do your best to put it on hold.

What you should be doing is striving for a better understanding of why you are the way you are and how you got that way—not finding a way to condemn others for the things that have gone wrong in your life or the fact that you don't have all the things you want. It's critical to come to terms with your personal history, but it is equally important to accept the fact that as an adult, unless you are trapped in a situation that involves some kind of ritualized brutality, you alone must take responsibility for your behavior now.

One of the lessons in life that is hardest for many of us to grasp is that our parents have limitations. One day, it will dawn on you that the people who raised you aren't the be-all and end-all of personal insights—they're only human. When this happens, it can be quite a shock, since up until that moment, every bit of your training has led you to trust their judgment on all things. But once you begin to see them as people who are just as fallible as anyone else, it not only opens the door for you to question their decisions, it makes it possible for you to trust your own.

Once you reach this point, you should be able to step outside the dynamics of the parent-child relationship and realize that your parents don't necessarily know any more than you do. They aren't necessarily experts on every subject. They can even be wrong. Learning to accept your parents as people is the first step toward becoming a healthy adult, because then you can love them and honor them but release them from blame. As long as they did the best they could do and kept your best interests at heart as well as they were humanly able, then the rest of your life is up to you.

CHAPTER TWO

Forget Fashion—Find Your Style

OKAY, LET'S SAY YOU'VE DECIDED that the best way to go about finding someone to love you for who you are is to be yourself. This may be easier said than done.

Who do you have to be in order to be desirable? Do you have to be thin? Do you have to be trendy? Do your eyebrows need to be tweezed just so and your cellulite "liposucked" until your thighs are as smooth and firm to the touch as an unripe plum? Must your nose be straight and your breasts perky? Do you need to accessorize, moisturize, abdominize, and downsize your thighs to find true happiness? We spend millions of dollars every year on fashion and beauty products in the hope that they will transform us into creatures of greater value to members of the opposite sex.

Many women allow themselves to be trapped in the mind-set that equates being attractive with submitting to every fashion trend that escapes the Paris runways, makes a detour through the Seventh Avenue knock-off shops, and eventually winds up on the racks at Kmart. If it's the style of the day, we think we have to wear it to be wonderful. Whether we're talking short-short skirts, push-up bras, Spandex, Lucite, screaming orange or lime pastel, L. L. Bean or The Gap—if fashion dictates, why should we argue? Why? Because even if these outfits do end up being halfway flattering, we come out looking as if we'd all been popped off the same cookie-cutter assembly line, or worse—for those of us who don't happen to be twenty-two years old, five-foot-seven, and a perfect size six—end up like mutant, space-alien wannabes or confused escapees from Ward Eight at Bellevue.

Think about your own wardrobe for a minute. Do you follow every new trend that comes along—even when the little voice in your head says it makes you look more geek than chic? Do you dress strictly to attract men at every hour of the day, even if you're just going out to the supermarket? Or do you hide your figure in baggy clothes and sensible suits so that you'll be taken "seriously"? When it comes to fashion, there are so many so-called experts out there telling us that we must do this and we must wear that or socially speaking we might as well be last week's leftovers, that it's small wonder many of us get our signals crossed.

Our culture spends so much time hinting that we women are in constant need of improving ourselves that even the most beautiful of us—the models and actresses who rightly or wrongly serve as our role models—have an ugly duckling tucked away somewhere in their psyches. We're bombarded from every glossy cover with the message that we're never good enough, pretty enough, well-dressed enough to grasp that brass ring (read: catch a man or keep him).

● ● ●

Kelly and Leigh are two women of passing acquaintance who often shared their morning commute. Kelly, a tall, platinum-haired, zaftig blonde, reminds many who meet her of Judy Holliday in *Born Yesterday*—only supersized.

She can usually be found wearing her idea of the closest thing to a "dress-for-success" outfit that her budget will allow, carrying a copy of the latest glamour magazine tucked into her bag. Kelly has so thoroughly bought into the line being spewed out by the spin doctors of contemporary design that she almost always accepts what they are selling, rather than thinking things through for herself.

Sadly, Kelly hasn't caught on to the fact that her tall, full figure often isn't appropriate for the clothes she chooses to put it in. Because she's so tremendously eager to please and fit in, she's taken some of her best assets and, rather than reveling in them and using them to her advantage (like a modern-day Mae West), she's turned them into setbacks. Kelly is afraid to question the authority of what fashion dictates is "normal," and, since she's not five-five and thin as a rail, she's continually dissatisfied with her appearance because there's no way she can conform to the standards of beauty that society has prescribed for her. It's a vicious cycle. The harder she tries to fit in, the more often she winds up looking like too much sausage strutting around in not enough casing. If she would just chuck the whole prepackaged image, trust her own judgment, and find what truly suited her, she'd be a knockout.

Leigh, on the other hand, doesn't give a fig for what she "ought" to put on, and only wears things she's at home in. "Fashions come and go," she says, "but I can't be bothered chasing every new trend. I know what I like and what's flattering to me. I wish other women would catch a clue. They'd be a lot happier."

To expand on her views, she recounts an incident that took place recently. Kelly had greeted her as usual while they stood waiting for their train and struck up a conversation, during the course of which she complimented Leigh on a pair of cowboy boots that Leigh happened to have on. They were acceptable cowboy gear to a New Yorker, though Leigh admits she knows for a fact that they wouldn't pass muster in Texas. They're weathered and worn at the heel, but she wears them anyway because they fit and because she likes them.

"You're so lucky those boots are brown," Kelly said.

"Why?" Leigh asked, not seeing where Kelly was going with this.

"Well," Kelly replied, lowering her voice to almost a whisper, "they go with everything."

(Says Leigh, "I had to concede that they did.")

"You know," continued Kelly wistfully, "I've got a pair almost exactly like them, but I can't wear them anymore."

"Do they hurt your feet?" Leigh inquired.

"No," she replied in dead earnest—"they're that olive color that was popular last year. I can't possibly wear them now. It's such a shame."

"Do you still like them?" Leigh wanted to know.

"Of course," Kelly said, "but you know . . ."

"Why don't you just wear them?" Leigh suggested. "I would."

"Well," said Kelly after a brief, contemplative pause, "that's true . . . but then, you've never cared much about style."

As soon as the words were out of Kelly's mouth, Leigh could see that she regretted them. "She hadn't meant to be insulting," Leigh explains, "she only felt sorry for me . . . but I felt sorry for her as well."

"No, Kelly," Leigh told her, "I care a great deal about style—it's *fashion* I don't give a damn about." And that, even if Kelly didn't understand her meaning, was the absolute truth.

• • •

As Leigh—and others lucky enough to be like her—know, every one of us is not only capable of finding our own, personal style, we owe it to ourselves to do so. Sure, it's hard dismantling the years of programming that have been piled on us by our parents, our peers, and the culture at large, but it's something that each of us needs to do in order to make friends with that face that looks back at us each morning from our mirror.

"Maybe as a result of having grown up in a somewhat Bohemian atmosphere," Leigh says, "I figured out a long time ago that I was not ever going to fit into the socially accepted standards of beauty in this culture, so for me, being 'normal' or fitting in was never something that I strove for. And this gave me a certain advantage: I didn't have to punish myself for not being magazine-pretty. I didn't base my self-esteem on the trend of the moment, or the pressure of my peers. I was comfortable in my own skin. My body, my clothes, my makeup and hair—much, at times, to the chagrin of my family, teachers, and other keepers of authority—were things always left up to me. And men still liked, desired, and even loved me. Not all men, of course, but then, I didn't like, love, or desire all of them either, so that seemed fair enough.

"But the oddest thing was that I never knew that I was different, that I'd been given a gift. I never tortured myself for not belonging on the page of anyone's catalogue. I just did pretty much as I pleased and let the chips fall where they may. I was who I was. I liked myself, and for the most part men turned up. No, not all the time, or in droves, but a steady flow that kept me fairly busy."

Sometimes, like everyone, Leigh hit a dating lull. But looking back on them now, she realizes that the times she had the fewest romantic prospects were at the points when she wasn't pleased with who she was. "If I wasn't dating, it usually had a lot more to do with me needing to figure out what wasn't working in my life, rather than my being disapproved of from exterior sources," she concludes.

It's really a no-brainer to figure out that no one is going to like her life 24-7, but as long as we like the people we are while we're living that life, things generally do work out.

So the next time you're overwhelmed by a sudden urge to go out and repaint your persona in someone else's image because you think your life has stalled and this will give you the jump start you need to fix it, resist the temptation. You'll be doing yourself a much greater service by sitting back down and concentrating on finding your own center instead.

It's like that story about the emperor's new clothes: It may take courage to fight the tide and speak out against the trendsetters, but in the long run, you can save yourself a lot of grief by learning to rely not on what others think of you, but on what you think of yourself.

CHAPTER THREE

The Five Senses

FROM THE TOP OF OUR HEAD to the tips of our toes, every-one has got an opinion on what makes for the body beau-tiful . . . and what doesn't. If you've got it—great. If not, life can be a hell on earth—if you let it be.

Even some of the world's great beauties and fashion models confess to having gone through that gawky, gang-ly phase when they were all angles and knees, braces and eyeglasses, stringy hair and bad skin—and even though they got over it, somewhere in the backs of their minds there always lurks that little voice that remembers them as geeks and doesn't hesitate to remind them of it when something pushes the insecurity button. But most of us are not fashion models. We don't have the luxury of wearing haute couture, having our outfits selected by a stylist, our makeup applied artfully by experts, and our hair coiffed by the genius of the day. But we do have choices. We can aspire to the standards of conventional beauty, or we can learn who we are and create our own.

In order for you to be your best possible you, you've first got to see yourself as you truly are. Now, this is not something that we can always accomplish between our-selves and our mirror alone. Both we and our favorite looking glass can be good at camouflaging the truth. Sometimes we need some help, so here's a little exercise to get you on track.

The Photo Shoot

For this exercise, you'll need either a camera with a self-timer and a tripod, or a friend to take the picture for you (you don't have to tell your friend what it's for if you don't want to, but a supportive friend can be a great help in this).

You're going to need a variety of shots taken from different perspectives, but don't worry if you don't have the most advanced camera on the market or if you're not the world's greatest shutterbug. Unless you have a background in photography (or the person taking the pictures has) your best bet is to take these pictures with natural light—as opposed to indoors with a flash. (Those pictures in which everyone's eyes look as if they're aflame with horror-movie demon blood are good for a laugh, but not much else.)

1. Before you begin, select a simple, neutral outfit to wear—a bodysuit and tights or a T-shirt and jeans are fine. Don't "do" your hair, just brush it out and wear it as you would normally. Don't put on anything but the most basic makeup (foundation and mascara, no more!).

2. First, take a series of head shots. Take a few from the front that frame your face and neck. (If your camera isn't adjustable for close-ups, just get in as tight as you can and still keep it in focus.) Don't pose or vogue for the camera. Try to keep your expression alert but relaxed. Now, take some shots of your profile that frame the face and neck. Be sure to get both sides of your face. Take a couple of shots of the back of your head to your shoulders. (Seriously! It's amazing how many of us neglect to remember that we are three-dimensional creatures, not two-dimensional drawings.) In order to size up the whole package, you have to look at the back as well as the front.

Finally, put on your makeup as you would to go to work or out for a casual evening and take a few more shots of your face and profile.

3. After you've got your head shots, take some full-body pictures. Follow the same procedure as before: take some head-on, some profile, and some from the rear. Try to get the camera far enough back so that all of you is in the frame (don't cut yourself off at the head or the knees!) and again, stand with your normal posture—don't pose, pretend, or suck in your gut. You don't have to show these snaps to anyone, and you don't even have to keep them when you're through. But remember, this is about getting to the real you, so just let her be.

4. When you get the pictures back from the developer, make an appointment with yourself to look at them and get to know the woman you'll be seeing. Set aside a specific hour or so when you can have the privacy and time you need to really digest the information that will be revealed to you. Pick a location where you won't be interrupted, whether it's your bedroom, the kitchen table, a nook in the library, or a booth in your local coffee shop. Bring a pad of paper and something to take notes with.

5. Now comes the hard part. As you look at the pictures, try to imagine that they are not you, but rather someone you've arranged to meet in the near future—kind of like a pen pal. As you proceed with this exercise, continue to think of "Ms. X" not as yourself, but rather as a woman with whom you'd like to be friends. By doing this, you'll be a lot less likely to be overly negative. Be descriptive in your writing. Don't just say a thing is "good" or "bad"—say what makes you think so.

6. Carefully examine the head shots one by one: first the face, then the profile, then the back. Take the time to look at them and give yourself a chance to let what they're telling you sink in. When you look at her face, what do you see in the expression? Is she at peace or is she anxious? Does she have "happy lines" around her mouth and eyes or tense furrows in her forehead? What are her best features? Eyes? Mouth? Cheekbones? Write down your thoughts. Next, write down what you think her most imperfect features are (remember not to be overly critical). Does it look as if she hasn't taken proper care of her skin? Is her nose too big? Is her chin too weak? Her lips too thin?

7. Now take out the shots with makeup and line them up with the bare-faced ones. Does her makeup accentuate her best features or detract from them? Does she make sure that her makeup doesn't stop at the line of her face (many women tend to think of their faces as a canvas, rather than a sculpture—the result being that they look as if they were wearing a mask). Does she look as if she is trying to compensate for one weak feature at the expense of the whole look?

(I'll never forget one lovely woman I once worked with. Not only was she was tall, model-thin, stylishly dressed, and extremely beautiful; she was down to earth, generous, and very talented, as well. Needless to say, I was, for the most part, in awe of her. But whenever we spoke face to face, something nagged at me about her appearance. Eventually, it dawned on me that it was her makeup. Somewhere in her life, she must have been told—and then convinced herself—that her eyes were "too close together." She attempted to compensate for this "flaw" by applying her eyeliner in a way that would have been great if she were about to step on stage, but was a little extreme for the office. Oddly enough, when she had some pictures taken by a professional photographer, she didn't insist that the makeup artist go the usual lengths with the liner. In the resulting photos, she looked absolutely stunning.

8. Now go back to the photos and check out the hair. Ask yourself, no matter how stylish the cut, does it suit her face? Does it set off her features to her advantage or does it overpower, downplay, or cover them up? Look at it from the front, the sides, *and* the back. Does it appear healthy? Don't forget, you should be taking notes on all of these things. Make a checklist with a brief summary next to each topic, so you can review them later.

9. When you're done with the head shots, take the full-body pictures and lay them out. The first thing you should look at is posture. How does this woman hold herself? What does her body language say about how she faces the world? Does she stand up straight and confident, or does she pull back and droop?

10. Okay, by now you're probably champing at the bit, so go for it: Write down everything about height, weight, and "problem areas" that you can think of. When you've finished, put the pictures away.

11. Now it's time to review your notes. If you've followed the true spirit of the exercise and written your comments as if the person in the pictures were *not* you but someone you're about to meet for the first time, the results probably aren't as bad as you thought they were going to be, are they? (If, however, your critique reads like a laundry list of complaints, you may want to set the whole thing aside, give yourself a break, and try it again at a later date. And the next time, do your absolute best to step *outside* of yourself as you make your observations.)

12. After you've read them through, give yourself a pat on the back for recognizing your strong points, then spend a few minutes reflecting on why these things please you and try to think of ways you can enhance those assets and let them shine. We won't spend a lot of time talking about your admirable qualities here. Most people don't need help with the good stuff, so let's see if we can lighten up some of that other baggage you're carrying around.

13. Go back over your list and pick out the one thing that you find most distressing. Though most of us are usually dissatisfied with several aspects of our outward appearance, let's start with one to use as an example. Say you don't like your nose. Maybe you wrote down that it looks like "a camel taking a nap." Now, take a moment to think about what you've written. Things like camels taking naps don't just pop into our heads from thin air, they come from somewhere.

Can you remember the first time you felt badly about whatever it is you've chosen as your "worst" flaw? Is it tied up with someone making a negative comment? If it is and you can identify the source, that's the first step in letting it go.

Yes, there are standards of beauty that have been accepted since the Roman times and even before, but that's just what they are—standards. There isn't just one type of beauty that is pleasing to the eye, and there's no reason to make yourself try to fit into someone else's mold—no matter how cruel or insensitive their behavior toward you.

There's a good chance that you've written down that the thing you are most dissatisfied with is your weight. Between the health clubs, diet regimens, exercise gurus, and aerobics fanatics pushing "do it yourself" weight loss and the plastic surgeons who promise to vacuum away your gallons of unwanted fat practically overnight, the American public is inundated with the ideal of thin, thin, thin. Judging from the rise in serious eating disorders in recent years, it's clear that women are the ones who truly take this subject to heart. We have begun to equate being overweight with being "losers," and that is a very dangerous precedent.

Using the Five Senses

Although human beings have five senses for perception, the one that we rely on the most to make judgments of both ourselves and others is sight. Let's face it—free will or not, we're fairly easily to brainwash. We want to fit in and we want to be accepted. So, if we are shown only a certain kind of image from the time that we're very young and taught that that image alone is what constitutes beauty, anything that deviates from that norm strikes us as odd or even ugly. And if we don't have the "right" look, many of us wind up feeling left out, less worthy, or even less lovable than our so-called prettier or thinner peers.

But think for a moment of your other senses. When it comes to hearing, taste, touch, and smell, we are much less likely to accept someone else's opinion as to what pleases us. Sure, we're all conditioned by our environment, and it's possible to acquire certain likes and dislikes, but it's a good bet that the multitudes won't be swigging down cod-liver oil cocktails at their trendy local *boite du soir* because it's suddenly become chic. The taste-buds are less easily intimidated than the eyes, and they have a habit of sticking up for themselves, too.

It's a shame that we can't value physical beauty in the same way we appreciate different smells. The world is full of limitless aromas and perfumes, but what to one person seems pure ambrosia to another is an ungodly stench. There are some women who adore the scent of rose oil, while others gag the minute they get within ten paces of it. Some men can't slather on enough cologne, while others prefer not to wear any. Cigar smoke? Some like it and some don't. Chestnuts roasting on an open fire? Again, not to everyone's taste. No one thing smells good to everybody—nor do we expect it to.

As you examine your list of negatives, try to pinpoint what it was that triggered each of your objections. Maybe it was a parent who only wanted you to be popular. Maybe it was a peer whose self-esteem depended on making others look bad to the rest of the group. Whatever the case, it's not the circumstances that are important here, but rather how you reacted to those circumstances, and learning to understand the behavior you may have developed as a result. If enough people tell us that something makes us undesirable, we end up believing them. But you don't have to accept the values and judgments of others if you don't want to. It is possible to define your own sense of beauty, and to live your life as that person. You can break the pattern, and once you do, you're going to like yourself a whole lot more. When you set a positive flow of energy in motion, you'll be surprised at how many healthy things will be drawn into that current.

So, now that you've gained some insight into why you are the way you are, here are a few pointers to help you find that road to your better self.

- **Make peace with being different—when you give yourself permission to deviate from the norm and still regard yourself as worthy of love, you are taking back your own power.**

If you live someplace that has a good museum nearby, I strongly urge you to take a trip there and spend the day. Study the varied faces of beauty that other cultures and other eras have embraced and celebrated. You will see that the feminine ideal has many forms. And while you may not be able to appreciate all the aesthetics, if you let

yourself tune in to the underlying feeling of joy and connection these images express, and learn to view beauty
with an open mind, you will be able to expand your definition of what acceptable is.

- **Be prepared to go through life knowing that people
  will make assumptions about you based on your
  looks, and be prepared to shatter those assumptions.**

It's always easier for people to judge us by what's on
the surface than by what's inside, especially in these days
of instant gratification, ten-second sound bites, and short
attention spans—but you don't have to let them get
away with it. You can have a big nose and still be a beautiful, remarkable woman. You can carry a few extra
pounds and still be attractive to men. Lead by example. If
you show those around you that you are unwilling to buy
into stereotypes, they will be a lot less willing to do so
when they are in your presence.

- **Do whatever you need to do to be your best self, but
  don't let others pressure you into being something
  you're not.**

Go back and take one last look at the list you've made.
If there are things about your appearance that you still
want to change, and you feel that by doing so you can
heighten your self-esteem, then go for it. Just be sure, as I
mentioned before we began this exercise, that you're
doing it for you and not for someone else.

I can't stress strongly enough that the most powerful
force of attraction we should strive to master is our own
attitude. Like who you are. Stand up straight and keep
yourself healthy. Do what makes *you* feel good and the
rest will follow, because there isn't just one type of beauty

in the world — beauty is without limits. And for every different shade, each unique variation, for every kind of beauty we personify, there is someone out there in the world who is going to appreciate that particular expression and love you for it.

CHAPTER FOUR

All the World's a Stage

IF YOU'VE EVER WONDERED why women spend so much time putting themselves together as if they were some kind of consumer product, the explanation is fairly simple. In our culture, it was set down long ago that the man was the shopper and the woman merely the "shoppee," whose place was on the shelf until that moment when she struck a fellow's fancy and he picked her up to read the label and examine the goods. Now, even at that point, it was at best a fifty–fifty shot that he'd actually toss her in the cart—along with his boxer shorts, power tools, jock itch medicine, and whatever other sundry purchases he might be making that day—take her to the salesclerk, and ring up the purchase, or, in other words, "make an honest woman of her." Men have a reputation for possessing short attention spans, and even gals who thought they were home free still ran the risk of Prince Charming finding something newer and shinier on his way to the checkout counter and tossing them back haphazardly to languish among the other day-old goods.

To combat this problem, and to guarantee that they would be the ones picked out instead of passed over, women found themselves having to resort to putting themselves in as attractive a package as possible and making all sorts of outrageous advertising claims, promising to so change a man's life for the better that the very thought of living without her would be intolerable.

It was hard to blame these women, since for most, the alternative was a lifetime of loneliness and ostracism.

But unfortunately, as these roles became more and more ingrained in the collective psyche of both men and women, the pattern of male as owner and female as property became accepted as the proper order of the universe. To be considered part of the community, you had to toe the line. But sadly, any system in which one segment of the population has all the power and the other has none always leads to abuse.

To function successfully in this environment, women were forced to be less than human — and to achieve security, they often had to resort to subterfuge. Being dependent on an oppressor not only for their happiness, but for the roofs over their heads, the beds they slept in, and the very food they ate, they found themselves in the position of doing, saying, and even thinking and becoming almost anything that suited the whim of the master in order to ensure their own survival. On the other half of this equation, men were taught that it was all right to dehumanize women, to trivialize their needs, to dismiss their ideas, and to discount their souls. It was all right to treat a woman badly because she really wasn't a person, she was a thing to be bought, sold, and owned.

That these roles endure today is not all that surprising, for a couple of reasons. First, power is seductive. Those who have it do not relinquish it easily, and those who have been taught to fear it do not take it up readily, doubting their own ability to keep from being overwhelmed by it. Propaganda, perhaps, but effective. Second, we get used to things. We get comfortable with our bad habits. We don't want to change. And this is true on both sides of the gender fence. Some women want nothing more than to give themselves into the care of a man and not to have to make any decisions. Some men don't want a soul mate—they want a combination "mommy–maid–play-thing" that they don't have to answer to.

Many women present themselves as a commodity, to be traded for the material things they want and the lifestyle they crave. Not that this is all that unusual. To one extent or another, we are all in the business of trading parts of ourselves to achieve the things we want. Whether it's our time, our talents, our looks, or even sex and love, we make deals in order to get what we want.

However, some women view the world with the eyes of a spoiled child, never understanding what it truly means to be an adult. The lesson they've missed is that while we are all due a certain amount of respect and con-sideration from the people around us, it shouldn't be at the expense of others. But sadly, many women are brought up to believe that the world is some giant psy-chodrama in which they are the star and the rest of the population—especially the men—are merely players. They never learn that while their own needs are valid, they are no more so than the needs of their lovers. When a man doesn't give them what they want the minute they want it, these women often construe it as mistreatment, which only fuels the dangerously overblown sense of entitlement that already drives their actions.

What follows is the story of a woman whose "ends-justify-the-means" tactics propelled her through life as if she were a demolition ball, and one man who was unlucky enough to cross her path.

• • •

Janine was raised by a father, a businessman who trav-eled extensively, and a mother, who believed that children were more ornamental than functional. By the time Janine went from diapers to dresses, she was already learning the art of performing pleasantly to garner the attention she craved. She'd figured out that when she was a pretty, precocious, talented child, she was rewarded, and when she was sad, frightened, or unruly, she was shunned. It wasn't very difficult for her to see which side of the bread the butter was on, so Janine always tried to show the world her "good" face and hide the "bad little girl" from view. Every once in a while, that other self would demand to be let out. When it did, Janine would "get sick," so although she temporarily lost favor, she did gain sympathy.

Janine observed her mother's behavior and the way her father reacted to it, and her understanding of how men and women were supposed to treat each other became skewed by the rituals inherent in their marriage. Time and again, she watched as her mother wound her father around her little finger, and he never knew what had hit him. Whether it was a new car or a fur coat, her mother would somehow lure him in, get him comfortable, stroke his ego, tempt him with the perfect sales pitch, steer him away from asking too many questions, camouflage her true intentions, and, in the end, even make him think that the whole thing had been his idea from the beginning.

When Janine became a teenager, her mother decided it was time she learned the tricks of the trade for catching a man. So she sat her down and told her the facts of life. Though the speech did include sex, it was not the main focus. "Sex and beauty are tools," her mother told her, "to be used wisely, not squandered." From what Janine could gather, catching a man was like playing blackjack. If a woman was to win consistently, the man must always be the gambler and the woman the dealer, or better yet, the owner of the casino. Janine was an adept and clever pupil. Under her mother's tutelage, and for want of other role models, she adopted her mother's advice and ways, took them to heart, and perfected them to a degree neither of them could have imagined.

When Tom met Janine, he thought she was the perfect woman. She was interested in his work, laughed at his jokes, catered to his whims, and always seemed able to meet life's little problems with a cheerful laugh. She truly seemed to enjoy his company but was always respectful when he needed his space. To the best of his knowledge, her own interests kept her schedule busy and her life full. Even though she didn't have a full-time job, she was, she told him, in the process of becoming an interior designer. *And with her great taste, why not?* Tom reasoned. She obviously had an eye for life's finer things, and her sense of style would have complemented the pages of any women's magazine.

When they first started going out, she held herself somewhat aloof, but Tom's curiosity was piqued by what he interpreted as her aura of mystery. He appreciated the fact that she wasn't one of those needy, demanding women who had the annoying habit of calling too often and wanting to discuss "the relationship." Janine customarily let Tom do most of the talking the first few months of their courtship, keeping her thoughts, emotions, and the intimate details of her past life very close to the vest. In fact, he used to tease her that she would make one hell of a poker player, and her response was, of course, that pretty little laugh he so delighted in.

Unlike so many women he'd dated after his divorce, she wasn't in a hurry to hop in the sack — even when he hinted at how badly he wanted her. But this only seemed to increase the intensity of his desire for her. Tom was the first to admit that he'd always enjoyed chasing gals who played hard to get. He liked the challenge. When the couple finally did wind up between the sheets, he felt as if he had won a prize, and the best part of it was that she made him feel as if he were the best lover in the entire world. She sighed, she moaned, she even went a little crazy; his every touch seemed to set off a firecracker of response in her. The first time she had an orgasm with him, it was unreal. Her cries of pleasure had been so loud, he didn't know how he'd face his neighbors—but he suspected it would be with a grin.

In three months, he was head over heels in love. In six, they were engaged. In less than a year, they were married, and Tom felt he was the luckiest man alive. Janine gave up her part-time job to concentrate on decorating the expensive condo he'd bought for them. She flew into a whirl of activity, making sure that everything from the carpet to the drapes to the towels and sheets was just right. Janine was in her glory and Tom had never been so happy. Each night over dinner, he recounted his day's conquests and she listened attentively. For the next half year, their life together met every one of his preconceived notions regarding marital bliss. Then, overnight, everything changed.

The good news was that Tom's firm was giving him a promotion. The bad news was that he was being transferred to a branch office almost two hours away by car. The four-hour commute each day was not something that Tom looked forward to, but it was no big deal, he reasoned. After all, the company had already promised to find them a great house and even pay the expenses of their move. And now that Janine had finished decorating their apartment—except for her constant tweaking and tinkering—it would give her the chance to move on to something on a grander scale, which he was sure would please her. Since Janine had always been the poster girl of the perfectly understanding wife, Tom felt certain that she'd stand by him no matter what monkey wrench fate might throw in their path, take it in stride, and even enjoy the challenge. But he was wrong.

"In one fell swoop, I felt as if I were married to a total stranger," Tom later explained in sadder-but-wiser tones. "She took off the velvet gloves and bared the surgical steel talons underneath. I knew she was crazy about our place in the city and that she might be upset about the prospect of having to give it up, but I never expected the reaction I got. She had always been so supportive. It was like someone flipped a switch and the woman I married was gone. Replaced by this . . . I'm sorry, this isn't a word I like to use, but it's the truth—she was a bitch."

"I'm not going anywhere," Janine informed him coldly when she heard the news. "My family is here, the stores are here. Really, I'm quite satisfied with our life as it is."

Tom sympathized with her. He offered to lease a car for her. He told her that though he would miss her, she could always spend a few nights a week with one of her friends in the city. Hell, he'd even consider buying a small studio apartment for her if she wanted to stay over, but it was as if he were talking to a brick wall. Janine would not compromise.

"I couldn't possibly disrupt my routine that way," she said. "What you're asking is out of the question. You'll just have to commute."

"Wait a minute, I found myself thinking," recalls Tom. *"She doesn't even have a job."* In fact, Janine had gone so far as to quit her design studies. She spent most of her time browsing the antique shops for the ultimate knickknack, having lunch with her girlfriends at trendy restaurants, and getting her nails done. Sure, there was always a picture-perfect dinner on the table when he got home from work. But he began to see her efforts for what they were. A picture. Something she'd seen in a magazine or a book.

"Suddenly I remembered an evening when she'd gone to bed with a terrible headache because a new recipe she was sure would be a knockout had failed to live up to her expectations," Tom relates. "Okay, it was inedible, but so what? 'We'll order take-out,' I told her. It was really no big deal, but she acted like it was some terrible tragedy. Eventually, I realized that everything had been an act with her. And I mean *everything*—right down to the theatrics in the bedroom."

When push came to shove, that's just what Tom got—the shove. He was out of there faster than you can say, "Heave ho." When their life went according to Janine's master plan, all was right with the world, but the minute the rules changed, so did Janine. For better or worse wasn't even the issue. Janine's problem boiled down to her need to be in total control, not only of herself, but of Tom as well, and when she could no longer do that, she no longer wanted Tom.

Tom, on top of being hurt, felt enormously cheated. "She made me think it was all up to me. I thought *I* was the one doing the pursuing. I thought *I* was the one calling the shots, but I see now that I was being manipulated the whole time. I never got to see the real Janine until it was too late."

The marriage lasted, from beginning to end, just under a year. Within four months of the final divorce decree, Tom received word through a mutual acquaintance that Janine had already gotten herself engaged to another man. "I feel sorry for the bastard," says Tom in earnest. "She put me through hell. It'll be a long time before I ever trust a woman again, and I can't begin to tell you what it's done to my sex life. Here she had me thinking I was this super-stud who could do no wrong, but now I can't stop myself from wondering if I was ever doing anything right. Not that it would have mattered to her. She would have put on the same show whether I was a baboon or the greatest lover who ever lived. My confidence is shot to hell."

• • •

Women like Janine are the stuff a million bad women-bashing jokes are made of. Look up "gold digger" in the dictionary, and there's her picture. Sure, in the big, bad world, a lot of people marry for reasons other than love, and as long as everyone is up front about it from the beginning, there's really nothing wrong with that. However, to play someone for what he's worth, rather than love him for who he is, is to reduce him to the status of a fool and yourself to the level of a common con artist — so it would be easy to paint Janine as the total villain of this piece, until we look a little closer.

On the surface, it's looks as though Tom's the one who got the short end of the stick, but in a way, though he got some pretty tough knocks, he's not the one who really comes out a loser. Sure, he took the easy road. He let his ego do his thinking for him — and he suffered the consequences. Maybe if he'd spent a little more time trying to delve deeper into Janine's character, he would have recognized her for the shallow pool she was. The bottom line? Next time, hopefully, he'll know better and make sure to look before he leaps.

Though when it comes to "next times," Janine will have a hard time doing anything different than carry on with business as usual. The other real downside to treating life as this game of taking someone for everything they've got is that, like the circus performer who balances a whole china cabinet's worth of spinning plates, sooner or later, something's gotta give. If Tom had known how to read them, he would have seen that Janine's headaches and tantrums were warning signs that she was losing control of her act.

Keeping up the pretense of being something you're not is hard, emotionally draining, soul-destroying work. If they're not careful, those who choose to take this road find out all too soon that the creature they've created to face the world can become a monster who guards the gate to truth and never lets it out at all. Eventually, the monster's personality will eclipse the other self altogether, leaving the soul to wither, perish, and be forgotten.

Janine never learned that a good man—one who treats you with love, fairness, courtesy, and most important, honesty—deserves the same treatment in return. Nor was it ever made clear to her that men are not toys or pawns or trophies any more than women are. They are people with feelings that must be taken into account and treated honorably. She was never shown that just because a man may not be able to give you what you want when you want it—if at all—it does not mean that he doesn't love you or is treating you badly, nor does it give you the right to punish him. In fact, Janine's education taught her the very opposite. And perhaps the saddest thing of all is that she has no idea what she's missing.

Does Janine know how to love anyone other than herself? No. Will she ever learn how? Probably not. Again, hers is a case of aiming for surface rather than substance, and in the long run that's a mighty thin diet to sustain a lifetime of love and commitment. Not only did she cheat Tom out of the woman he thought he'd married, she cheated herself out of ever attaining the kind of love that comes from letting someone know the inner you—the good, the bad, and the ugly—and accepting you, flaws and all.

On the opposite side of the coin from women who think they need to sell themselves are the men who think they can buy you. (Yes, they're still out there!) Too bad none of them are labeled. It would save the rest of us a lot of grief. For example, here's a cautionary tale from Liz, a thirty-two-year-old veteran of the dating dance.

• • •

"Women don't really need their egos," her date, Chris, told her confidently as they sat sipping tea on the picturesque patio of an outdoor restaurant nestled in the heart of the botanical garden. It was a lovely afternoon in late spring. Nearby, the Bronx River, swelled by seasonal rain, sped briskly along its course. Her companion, Liz had learned only after their rendezvous began, was a devotee of "the men's movement."

Says Liz, "I remember thinking, as he unfolded his many-layered philosophy regarding what he considered to be ideal conduct between men and women, that the stream wasn't the only thing babbling."

Still, while in her opinion his views perhaps would have found their best use fertilizing the nearby flower beds, she let him continue. For, truth be told, she couldn't help but be fascinated — kind of in the way that you can't stop yourself from gaping at a hideous traffic accident on the side of a highway.

"And why is that?" she asked, trying to keep the tone of her voice level, caught as she was between simultaneous impulses to run screaming, whack him over the head with a mallet, or laugh with such force she was sure to snort tea out through her nose.

"Well," he replied thoughtfully, "the man is the one who has to be out there every day, in the thick of things. He's the one who has to be the aggressor when it comes to business."

"But women have to work, too," Liz pointed out.

"Ah, but a businesswoman can afford to bend and not be viewed as weak," Chris replied with authority. "As a matter of fact, you ladies are expected to back down in the workplace. A woman's greatest strength is her ability to compromise."

"And a man's greatest strength?" she felt compelled to ask, even as she felt her spine bristle at the "you ladies" reference.

"To be able to go for the throat. A guy has to be a real killer to be successful," he concluded.

"But surely every human being needs to have their own identity?" she pressed.

"Not really," he maintained. "You see, I believe that if the sexes went back to living the way nature had *intended*, women would have absolutely no need for identities of their own. In nature, women are like the moon and men are like the sun."

"Excuse me?" she nearly spat, beginning to wonder if there was any chance of snagging a mallet at the concession stand.

"Men create the light, women merely reflect it. Women don't really have identities without men to define them."

"You mean I exist only in the context of how I'm perceived by the men in my life?"

"Exactly."

Liz had been wrong, this was no traffic accident, this was the *Titanic*. But since she'd already hit the iceberg, she decided to go with the flow. "So," she inquired dubiously, "what are you hoping to find in your next relationship?"

"I'm really ready to get married," Chris confided, "so I guess what I'm looking for is the perfect wife."

Now this *should be interesting.* "Could you define what you mean by perfect?" Liz asked earnestly. She could tell by the way he answered that he'd put a lot of thought into this one.

"As I see it, a woman's role is mainly one of comfort. If I come home after a hard day's work, I want someone who will listen to me and be sympathetic. I don't want to be met at the threshold with a bunch of problems or irritations. I just want to relax."

"But what if your wife's had a bad day, too?"

"I don't think it's asking too much that she keep it to herself. After all, I'm providing her with a house and money. I don't see why it's such a big deal for you women to have our dinner in the oven, a drink for us in your hand, and a smile on your face when we men walk through the door."

"I take it that this wife of yours won't be working?"

"No," he replied indignantly. "Why should she? I'm going to give her everything she needs."

I'll bet, she thought. "But what if the woman you meet has work that makes her happy? Maybe she'll have a job that gives her a sense of who she is."

"But don't you see? Once we're married, she'd be getting all that from me."

By now, she could feel the clouds of a nasty headache gathering ominously behind her eyes, but like an old trooper who keeps on hoofing while the theater burns down around her, Liz forged onward. "And all she has to do is give up her ego."

"Right!"

"So, in return for the material things — the house, the car, and spending money — all she has to do is be a perfect homemaker, a perfect sounding board for you, a perfect mother to your kids (God forbid another generation like this one!), keep her problems to herself, and perform in whatever role you define for her?"

"Yes. Doesn't that make sense?"

Sure, she thought, *if you're trapped in a 1950s sitcom. Lucy, I'm home. . . .* "Well," Liz said, deciding to pull out all the stops, "what about sex?"

"What about it?"

"Let's just say for the sake of argument that you find this beautiful wife who happily accepts the terms of your generous bargain. What if it turns out she's not so hot in the sack department? What if down the road you get bored in the bedroom?" Catching her drift, he leaned in and replied with a conspiratorial smile, "You know how men are. I'd just have an affair. It wouldn't mean anything."

"And what if she got bored with you, could she 'just have an affair,' too?"

"Of course not! No wife of mine . . ."

And there it was, the operative word —*mine*. He owned her. She was property. And Liz, poor thing, had a crazed woodpecker with a hydraulic jackhammer pounding in her head. She recalls, "My neck seized up, my temples pounded with a high-pitched trombone solo—even my teeth hurt. Suddenly, I was filled with the urge to chop something up in little bits—preferably something raw and bloody." The date was over and Liz was ready for what she likes to call beef-stew therapy, but she still managed to smile.

"And I wish you all the luck in the world finding her," she said, rising to leave.

"You're going?"

"Yes. I'm sorry, Chris, but I'm a little too attached to my ego right now to give it up for a man. No hard feelings."

"Well, at least let me drive you home," he offered. "It's starting to rain." She had to say one thing for him— he was a gentleman.

"No, that's all right, I have to make a stop on the way and I don't want to hold you up." After they parted company, Liz headed to her local supermarket, purchased a beautiful slab of beef, some carrots, mushrooms, potatoes, and fresh spices, popped into the liquor store for a bottle of burgundy, then walked home, damp but defiant, to spend the rest of the afternoon dicing her way back to mental well-being.

"But," she confesses, "as I peeled and pounded, sliced and smashed, dredged and browned, I couldn't help but think about all the advice my married girlfriends had given me about finding a mate. Chris had been quite handsome and, at least in an old-fashioned sense, chivalrous. He had pulled out my chair and paid for my meal. He held down a high-profile job and took home a high-profile salary. He had a nice car and nice clothes. On a physical level, we found each other attractive — and to top it off, he really wanted to get married. Was I letting a good one get away? Surely many of my friends would have thought so.

"I realized," she continues, "that in some cosmic way, I had just been offered my shot at the jackpot and had folded my hand without even putting an ante on the table. Who knows? Had I played my cards right, I could have taken the pot. Of course, if I'd wagered on this particular game and won, I'm fairly sure that I would have either wound up in a loony bin or on death row for murdering the pompous ass.

"Still, by my friends' standards, this guy was a real catch. He could have provided me with all the material things I'd ever need, and all I'd have to give up to get them was my soul."

● ● ●

Maybe the bargain Liz was offered was a good one back in our grandparents' time. For a lot of women, maybe it was the only game in town, but today, though it might be a viable choice for some, it doesn't have to be the choice for anyone who doesn't want it to be.

You don't have to buy into the hype. You don't have to buy into the fear. You don't have to buy into the loneliness. And you don't have to play the games to have a successful, long-term relationship. You don't even have to have a long-term relationship if you don't want one.

Shhh—don't tell granny, but you don't have to get married to be happy—or to consider yourself a success as a woman. Life isn't about one choice, it's about lots of choices—grand passions, small intimacies, deep pleasures, and endless opportunities.

You can have what you want. And what you want can change. As a matter of fact, it probably will, but even if you make mistakes or decide to swap horses midstream, if you go through life liking who you are, then you're in for a pretty pleasant and enlightening ride. Maybe you'll end up at some destination other than the one you had in mind, but that can be okay too. Hell, sometimes, it's even better.

If you've taken the lessons in Part One to heart, it's time to move ahead and apply them to the pursuit of love and romance. Don't worry if you haven't gotten everything down pat. There isn't going to be a final exam. No one ever knows all the answers, and the only people who get it right 100 percent of the time are in the movies.

What life *will* throw you, however, is a series of pop quizzes. But that's no reason to panic. With enough time and practice, you'll find yourself becoming more and more comfortable with both your social and romantic skills. The hardest thing to manage during the course of this process of change and discovery is remembering to keep on being yourself. That may sound like a contradiction, but it really isn't.

Let's get back to pastry for a minute. Think of yourself as the piecrust. Some days, you'll need more water, some days more shortening. There are times when the recipe will require some salt, and others when a touch of sugar will be what's called for—but no matter how you roll it out or what way you bake it, it's still essentially piecrust. Time, trial, and error will only work in your favor. And the more often you bake, the sooner you'll figure out which texture, flavor, and filling are right for you.

PART TWO

The Art of Romance

CHAPTER FIVE

The Ten Principles of Dating

ONCE YOU'VE ACCEPTED the rightness of loving yourself—
or at least gotten a jump on it—you'll be ready to meet,
mingle, and mix it up with members of the opposite sex
in a positive way. There is no guarantee that the next man
you meet will be "the one." But no matter what the outcome of your future romantic encounters—whether it's a
one-week fling or a lifelong love affair—when you
approach dating from a self-confident perspective, you
have the best chance of attaining real happiness for yourself and creating it for your lover.

Does this mean you're never going to be hurt again?
No. Does it mean that you won't make mistakes or even
change your mind and decide you want to pursue other
choices? No. But to say that fulfillment and everlasting
love can only be achieved by following one narrow,
0predetermined path is to live in a fantasy land. No one
can, or should, make those promises to you, because no
one can truly keep them. Happiness is an ephemeral,
mutable thing, and just as we must outline our own
parameters of beauty, so too must each of us define what
makes us happy.

If you're one of those people who find themselves making a thousand and one excuses not to pursue relationships

because of the fears I've just mentioned, you've got one more chore to do before you get started. Take a climb up into that dark attic of your psyche, find the inner fuse box to your negativity generator — it's a good bet it's hiding behind all that dusty baggage from your adventures in "Coulda-Woulda-Shoulda-Land" — and throw the switch to "Off." Got it? Good. Think you're ready for the fun part? You are — almost.

Instead of thinking "rules," think "basics." Before plunging into the man/woman/dating thing, there are some basic principles of courtesy and self-protection that every smart woman should follow. Love is a bit like flying a plane: once you know what you're doing, you can hop in and go anywhere you want — but even a simple joyride can turn into a disaster if you don't know the fundamental laws of aviation. Before you head out into the wild blue yonder, consider the following top ten list of basic dos and don'ts, so that no matter what flight plan or weather conditions fate sends your way, you'll always be prepared.

1. Go for what you want.

Radical as this may sound to some, there's nothing wrong with seeing something you want and going after it — even, or especially, if what you want is a particular man. No one is suggesting that you should slip your would-be paramour a sedative, drag him back to your apartment, and force him to be your love slave. But just because you're willing to make the first — or even second and third — moves, you needn't worry that you're going to wind up like the Glenn Close character in *Fatal Attraction*. Confidence and self-assurance are sexy. You may have to learn to fine-tune your levels of assertiveness, but this is something that comes with practice. As long as you keep things casual and don't lead anyone on, it's perfectly acceptable to cast your net, even if at some point you're going to toss back the catch of the evening.

Says Rhonda: "I got married really young—at sixteen. About ten years into the marriage, we called it quits. My husband Brian and I had practically grown up together. We were going steady by the time we were twelve. So, there I was, twenty-six years old, on my own for the first time, and I realized that I didn't know the first thing about dating! I was appalled by how clueless I was, but determined to get back into the swim—if I could just figure out how to do it without drowning, that is.

"Fortunately, I still knew a lot of women who were single at the time, and they offered to help me get my feet wet—and not get in over my head, so to speak. The first night we all went out, I just sat in the corner like a timid little mouse. I could barely bring myself to even look at a man, but with the encouragement of my friends, eventually I came out of my shell.

"On our third 'Girls' Night Out,' I spotted a very attractive man at the end of the bar. We made eye contact. He smiled. A minute later, the bartender came over and said that the gentleman would like to buy us a drink. We accepted, and the gentleman joined us. He was a lovely man, an appliance salesman named Bill. He and I spent the rest of the night flirting and chatting, and although we weren't really in tune, we enjoyed each other's company all the same. And I have to admit the attention bolstered my ego.

"The next weekend, I was at the library, helping my son do some research for a homework assignment. I'd asked the librarian if she might recommend a good book on dinosaurs. She wrote down a title and catalogue number, then sent me off with some rather vague instructions and a wave of her hand. Five minutes later, I still couldn't find the book and was headed back to the desk when I

happened to see a very handsome man sitting in the peri-
odical section, reading a *Smithsonian* magazine.

"I remember thinking, *Hmm, he's probably interested in science, maybe he can help me find my dinosaur book.* But the truth was, I was interested in finding out about him, so I walked up and said, 'Excuse me, I hate to trouble you, but I have no idea where this book might be.' I handed him the card the librarian had given me. 'Can you point me in the right direction?'

"He took the card and looked it over, then said, 'This is good, but I know a better one. I'll be happy to show you where they are.' We started to talk and I found myself very attracted to him. He had a great sense of humor and a pair of beautiful, hazel-colored eyes behind his glasses. When we got to the shelf with the books I needed, he showed me the three that would be of most use to my son. 'I guess I should be getting back to my *Smithsonian*,' he said. 'If you need any more material, come and get me. I'll be here for another half an hour.'

"'Listen, I should be done by then,' I told him. 'You've been such a big help, I'd like to say thanks. Can I buy you lunch?'

"'I'd like that,' he replied. Thirty minutes later, we were sitting over two B.L.T.s and cherry Cokes at the local diner. It was great fun. We've gone out a few times since, but I'm not in any hurry to leap into another major commitment so soon. I'm just taking each day as it comes and enjoying the opportunities."

2. Follow "the Golden Rule."

"Do unto others as you would have them do unto you"? Yup. Men may be from Mars and women from Venus, but we all have feelings that need to be respected, values that must be taken into account, and dreams that deserve to flourish. If you are a liar, how can you expect love to bring you the truth? If you are a thief, how can you hope for love to trust you with its most valuable gifts?

Lola's is a case in point: A beautiful girl, Lola spent her entire life coasting on her good looks. She never thought about anything except gratifying her own needs, and never took responsibility for her actions. On the road of romance, Lola was like a hit-and-run driver who always managed to charm her way out of a ticket and then speed away, trouble-free . . . and then she met Theo.

Theo knocked her totally for a loop. He had it all—a great mind, flashy car, an impressive bank balance, and on a physical level, she'd never been so attracted to anyone before. *This is it*, she told herself, *I could actually fall in love with this man*. So, Lola put her tried-and-true formula in motion and waited for the inevitable results.

With her striking good looks, she had no trouble getting Theo's attention, and in due course, he asked her out. For a while, things went swimmingly, and Lola couldn't have been more pleased. She allowed events to take their natural course, plying her stratagems and biding her time until the moment when she would reel in her catch.

On several occasions, when she felt that Theo had behaved inappropriately—either by asking her out without enough advance notice, or by being unavailable when she thought they should have plans—Lola firmly "put him in his place." The fact that she had to fabricate reasons and circumstances in order to do so didn't faze her in the least. In fact, lying and manipulating to get what she wanted were so ingrained in Lola's behavior that they weren't second nature—she'd allowed them to become her nature.

Then one evening about three months into their relationship, disaster struck . . . at least for Lola. They were dining at an elegant French restaurant when a very lovely woman walked by their table. "Pam," Theo called out to

her, "how are you?" The woman stopped and Theo introduced her to Lola.

As they chatted amiably, Lola's blood began to boil.
I'll nip this in the bud, she vowed, smiling through
clenched teeth.

After a moment, Pam said she had to be going. "A
pleasure to meet you," she said to Lola.

I'll bet, you man-stealing witch, thought Lola, but
replied, "For me, as well. I hope we see you again soon."

"Yes," said Theo, "it really has been too long. I'll call
you next week, okay?"

"That would be terrific," Pam answered. "I'll look forward to it." By this time, Lola was seething, but she managed to retain a calm veneer.

"Pam's a great gal," Theo remarked.

"I suppose so," Lola countered coolly, "if you like *that*
type."

"What do you mean?" Theo wanted to know.

"Well," said Lola, launching into a calculated tale, "I
didn't want to say anything while she was standing here,
but I happen to know that girl's a home wrecker. No
morals whatsoever."

"Really?" said Theo, seeming genuinely surprised.

"As a matter of fact," Lola continued smoothly, "she
stole one of my best friend's husbands, then dumped him
five months later, just like that," snapping her fingers to
punctuate her point.

"You don't say," replied Theo. "And when was this?"

"Last year about this time," she concluded, confident
that Theo had swallowed her story hook, line, and sinker.
During the rest of the meal, Theo was quieter than usual,
but still attentive. When he drove Lola to her apartment,
she decided to end the evening by letting him have sex
with her, so she invited him upstairs, but he begged off,
pleading, of all things, a headache.

Twenty minutes later, Lola's phone rang. It was Theo. "Lola," he said, "I can't see you anymore."

"It's that Pam woman, isn't it?" Lola demanded angrily.

"In a way. Look, Lola, I guess I should have stopped you when you were talking Pam down in the restaurant, but I just couldn't believe my ears."

"You're in love with her, aren't you?" Lola practically spat.

"Well, I do love her . . ."

"You bastard!" Lola hissed.

"Lola," said Theo in as even a tone as he could muster, "Pam's my cousin. I hadn't seen her in over two years — she's been doing relief work in Africa."

"What?" she gasped.

Theo repeated what he'd just said. "She's my cousin. I can't believe the lies you made up about her. Girl, you need some serious help, and I hope for your sake you get it." Then he hung up, leaving Lola with nothing but dead air.

Not everyone is a great believer in karma, but the saying "What goes around, comes around" is true more often than not. Maybe we don't always have the personal insight to recognize when that cosmic watchdog is biting us on the butt, but he's there, and man, are his teeth sharp! So, if you want kindness, be kind. If you want respect, then be respectful. Think about how little you like to be manipulated the next time you're planning to get over on a man who strikes your fancy. Maybe you'll think twice.

3. Be honest.

Being honest means being yourself, and sometimes that can be hard, especially at the beginning of a relationship. Because we want people to like us and worry that we aren't good enough, smart enough, charming enough, hip enough, pretty enough, or *whatever* enough, many women put on a facade that we *think* will make us more appealing. The problem we encounter when we undertake such a venture is that no matter how good our intentions, these little acting exercises have a nasty habit of blowing up in our faces.

Marta, a twenty-four-year-old postgraduate student, recounts this recent experience: "One day, I had some time to kill between classes so I decided to go for a walk. All of a sudden, it started to rain, so I ducked into a coffee shop. Unfortunately, everyone and his Aunt Frances must have had the same idea, because there wasn't a seat in the house. I was about to go back out and brave the elements, when this really cute guy waved at me and motioned for me to join him.

"*Why not?* I thought. So I walked over and sat down. Turns out he was a jazz musician, a sax player. As we sat sipping cappuccino he told me about his music and I listened attentively, as if each word that passed his lips was a pearl. Now the truth was, I didn't know the first thing about jazz and I'd never really taken any interest in it, but I wanted him to like me, so I pretended that I was interested. He asked me out on a date for Saturday and I accepted. By then, it was time for me to head to class, so we exchanged numbers, picked a place to meet, and said good-bye.

"Saturday at six-thirty, I was waiting for him by the predetermined landmark. He strolled up and said Hi, then told me he'd gotten tickets for a great show downtown—a tribute to 'Bird.' Now, the only bird I knew anything about was Big Bird, but being with him was pleasure enough for me, so I didn't have to feign enthusiasm for the evening's plans. By the time we got on the subway, I knew I was in over my head. He was tossing off jazz terms and spewing out names, and I was totally lost, but I kept nodding, trying to look thoughtful, getting myself in deeper and deeper.

"Eventually the topic turned to female vocalists, and he mentioned that Lady Day was his favorite. *At last,* I thought, *someone I know something about!* My dad adored Doris Day, and I just assumed that was who he meant. So the next thing I piped up with was, 'Yes, and didn't you just love her in *Please Don't Eat the Daisies?'*

"My date started to laugh, like I'd made some joke. I just giggled nervously. I think it was then that it dawned on him that I didn't know Billie Holiday from New Year's Day. 'Do you like Ella?' he asked, all innocence.

"'Yes, she's great,' I found myself saying.

"'Maybe we can go see her next concert,' he offered.

"'That would be wonderful,' I told him.

"'Of course it might be hard to get tickets,' he went on. 'She's playing a very exclusive room.'

"'Really? Which one?' I asked.

"'Heaven,' he replied sarcastically. 'She's dead, you know.'

"The rest of the evening . . . well there really wasn't one. I was so mortified, I told him I suddenly wasn't feeling well and had to go home. He didn't argue. Let me tell you, I'll never pull a stunt like that one again!"

If you make yourself over into something you're not—or pretend to be—to win a man's affections, sooner or later he'll figure out that you're not what you seem, and if he has anything more than half a brain, he'll be out of there faster than you can say jump. Of course, if he has less than half a brain, he may stick around, but would you really want him?

4. Be open.

Do men love a mystery? Sure, who doesn't? But that doesn't mean you need to keep your thoughts, opinions, and feelings to yourself. Being open has two benefits. First, on an intellectual level, a woman who can express what she's thinking is bound to be more entertaining and intriguing than one who simply parrots back what a man says to her. It's like the difference between playing tennis with a backstop and with a human being. Though the first method is good for practice, there's no real excitement in batting a ball against a batch of bricks. But a good game against a worthy opponent can be stimulating, challenging, and downright thrilling. So talk it up!

Second, men aren't mind readers. They want to know what you're thinking. They want to know what pleases you, so that they can try to satisfy your preferences if it is within their power to do so. They also want to know what displeases you so that they can avoid stepping on land mines. But unless you tell them what you want, and let them know where your limits lie, don't expect the knowledge to just pop into their minds like Athena springing from the head of Zeus. While some insightful men can figure it out, most of them need some directions from you. This isn't a failing on their part, so when you start dating a man, consider yourself new territory and don't be afraid to hand him a road map.

That's what Sonya did, and she reports that the results couldn't have been better. "I come from a large family," she relates. "Three boys and four girls. My mom and dad are both professors at the state university — she's philosophy, he's literature. It was always a big deal for our family to get together over dinner and discuss not only the events of our day, but what was on the nightly news, world politics, the stuff we were studying in school. Everyone was encouraged to speak up, and we all got into the habit. It made for some lively discussions and heated debates, and I look back on those times as some of the best in my life.

"The other challenge you have to deal with in a big family is making sure everybody's needs get met. It was a big balancing act, but somehow my parents managed it really well. Part of the way they accomplished this was to have a weekly meeting where we all aired our views and outlined the things we wanted. Of course I didn't need a pony when I was six, but my parents let me tell them why I thought I should have one. Then, after they'd let me express myself and really listened to me, they explained to me about zoning laws and made me understand just how much time, work, and money goes into keeping a pony. We wound up with a dog instead.

"As an adult, I've carried this forthright manner into my relationships. Yes, some men couldn't handle it, but they were wimps—either emotionally or intellectually. I dated lots of guys who loved my mind and my 'fat mouth,' who didn't find me intimidating in the least. Eventually, I even married one of them."

Now, there are pundits out there who might try to sell you on the idea that men are too limited—at least in the beginning of a relationship— to be interested in ideas that don't jibe with their own, or to be able to process emotional information of too serious a nature. And the truth is, some of them can't, but ask yourself, is a man who is unable, or unwilling, to wade in beyond his knees when it comes to emotions really someone you'll be able to count on to help shoulder the burden when life throws something heavy at you? Or will he simply sidestep the problem and leave you holding the bag?

Of course, trust takes time, but if you're getting the impression that a man you're interested in hasn't been in touch with his own feelings since the Ice Age, and immediately freezes up when you talk about your own, there's a good chance that he's not ever going to change. Men who habitually avoid emotional intimacy aren't suddenly going to open up once you've 'got them hooked,' and you may have your work cut out for you trying to differentiate between the merely cautious and the hard case. But it's definitely worth the effort. A lover who isn't interested in your mind or your feelings isn't someone you should be bothering with in the first place. If he's simply looking for a woman whose views are a complimentary reflection of his own, you're better off handing him a mirror and letting him date himself.

5. Trust your common sense.

We all have that little voice in our heads that tells us when something is not right, but a lot of times we don't listen to it because we think it's our fear talking, trying to hold us back. And while it's true that those two voices may sound similar, if you listen carefully, they are singing two entirely different tunes. If you find yourself in a situation where you are not appreciated, don't waste your time thinking things are going to change. Move on.

When Becky met Ray she thought he was the bee's knees. She'd just moved to a new town, and one Friday night her office-mates dragged her out to the local watering hole. There behind the bar stood Ray — charming, handsome, quick with a joke, and ever-so-attentive. Becky developed an instant crush, but did her best to keep her feelings to herself.

While she was reapplying her lipstick in the ladies' room, one of her coworkers remarked, "Gee, Ray really seems to like you."

"You think?" Becky asked incredulously.

"He hasn't taken his eyes off you all night," her chum replied.

"Really?" Becky pressed.

"Really."

Armed with new confidence, Becky went back out to the bar and began to flirt a little more aggressively, and Ray just ate it up—though something at the back of her mind was nagging at her, telling her that things seemed a bit too easy. Something about Ray's responses just didn't feel right, but Becky put her reservations on the back burner.

It was getting late and her friends wanted to leave, but Becky was determined to stay. "I'll cab it home," Becky told them.

"Sure you will," said her comrade from the ladies' room, giving her a knowing wink. "See you Monday." Then she gave Becky a quick hug and whispered happily, "And I'll want to hear *all* the details."

Becky laughed and told her she'd be the first to know. After her friends had gone, Becky sat at the nearly empty bar talking with Ray. Within an hour, the rest of the customers were gone.

"Time to lock up," Ray told her.

"I guess I should call a taxi," Becky said wistfully.

"Becky, honey, I know this sounds corny, but I feel like someone who's been sleeping all my life, dreaming of something beautiful and never finding it. Now here you are—my living dream. Please come home with me tonight."

"I'd love to," she told him. Even in the midst of all the magic, a wake-up call was trying to reach her brain, but instead of picking up, she let her mind take a message.

That night, they made love for hours. Ray was the most skilled and expert lover Becky had ever been with. No man had ever touched her as appreciatively or made her body sing with more pleasure. The next morning, he called a cab for her and paid the driver in advance. "See you soon, dream girl," he said, giving her one last, deep kiss.

Once she was home, Becky realized that in all the excitement, she had forgotten to give Ray her number, and much to her chagrin, she hadn't ever asked him his last name. *No big deal*, she told herself. *I can call him at work*. Then she had a better idea. Ray had mentioned that he was filling in for the regular Saturday bartender tonight. Why not show up at the end of his shift and surprise him? Why not indeed.

At two-thirty in the morning, she arrived at the bar, which was deserted except for Ray . . . and a leggy, buxom blonde whose hand he was holding across the counter. The two were so wrapped up in each other, they didn't even see her come in. Then she heard Ray tell the blonde, "Please don't go, baby. I know this sounds corny, but I feel like someone who's been sleeping all my life, dreaming of something beautiful and never finding it. Now here you are — my living dream. Please come home with me tonight."

Before the blonde could answer, Becky marched over, picked up the woman's drink, and emptied its contents straight into Ray's face. Then, turning to the woman, she said, "Honey, he says that to all the girls — and I do mean *all* of them." Then she stormed out, hailed a cab, and went home.

As she lay in bed trying to sleep, her mind finally got a chance to replay the message it had been so urgently trying to send her the night before. She realized that instead of listening to her inner warning systems, she'd allowed herself to fall for a slick line. *Too good to be true*, the message ran. *Too good to be true!*

6. Have reasonable expectations.

Are you looking for instant gratification? Prince Charming with a Gold Card and an unlimited line of credit? A virile genius who will wave his magic wand in your general direction and "Poof!" all your problems will disappear? The odds of any of this happening are pretty slim. Men do not exist in the world merely to "fix" us, complete us, or please us—and it does no one a service to expect that just by having a man in your life, suddenly everything will be a sunshine-and-roses, carefree ride.

"Did ya ever see that movie, *Mystic Pizza*?" asks Melinda. "The one where Julia Roberts plays this small-town girl who lands herself a millionaire? Well, for some reason, I was sure the same thing was going to happen to me! Can you imagine? I was working as a waitress by day, dreaming of Prince Valiant at night. Lots of really great fellas asked me out, and once in a while, I'd go, but none of them ever measured up to the fantasy man I'd concocted in my head, and eventually, they all threw up their hands in disgust and went after women who were a little more based in reality.

"Looking back at it now, I can't blame them, but at the time, I was determined to strike it rich, find true love, and never have to work another day in my life. Okay, so I was delusional. But if it could work for Julia, why couldn't it work for me? Why? Well, mostly because there weren't too many millionaires—or even guys with steady pay-checks—coming into the diner. And when one who seemed even a remote possibility did, they invariably wanted a burger deluxe, no waitress on the side, please. To top it off, the rich-looking guys were always the worst tippers!

"After a few years of this self-defeating scenario, I met Ricky—a nice guy, with a decent job, a full head of hair, and two kids from a former marriage. We got along great and over the course of the next few months became really good friends. One day, Ricky stopped by after work, sat down at the counter, and ordered his dinner to go. We were just shooting the breeze, like always, when the subject of romance came up. So I told him my whole *Mystic*

Pizza plan, and how I knew that one day a really rich guy was going to walk through the door and sweep me off my feet. I half expected him to look at me like I was crazy, but he just smiled — and ordered a cup of coffee.

"Now that was odd, because as a rule, he didn't touch the stuff, but I got it for him anyway. Instead of drinking it, he just inhaled the aroma. "It's just what I thought," he said, then he pushed the cup back across the counter toward me.

"'Something wrong?' I asked, but he just kept grinning that sweet grin of his. Finally, I bent over and took a deep whiff myself.

"'About time you did that,' he said gently. I didn't get it. 'Wake up and smell the coffee, honey. You could meet a rich man, marry him, and he could lose all his money a month later, or you could find someone who really loves you and fill your life with the richness that really counts.'

"Then I saw that this man — my best friend — was in love with me. He was offering me a chance for something real. Did I take it? You bet your ass I did, and even though I still have to work, I've never been sorry one day in my life."

7. Be flexible.

Love is not a military maneuver. Romance is not a religious cult. If you think there is only one "right" way to do things, that makes every other kind of behavior "wrong." Having to have your way all the time is not a sign of strength, it's a sign of weakness and inflexibility. No one died and left you queen. You are not four years old. Wake up and smell the coffee. Do you remember that fable of Aesop's about the oak tree and the reeds? If not, let me update it for you. . . .

• • •

On the shore of a river stood a mighty oak tree named Ms. Thing. She was tall, proud, and very beautiful. A little way down by the bank grew a stand of slender, graceful reeds—the Marsh sisters.

Now, truth be told, Ms. Thing didn't think too highly of her more supple cousins, the Marshes. Every time Mr. Breezy would blow through the neighborhood, they would bend to him with a tolerant curtsy, dance a lively little two-step in his arms, then wave politely as he was leaving and go back about their business. Why, it rattled Ms. Thing's leaves just to think about it. "Imagine giving in to a man like that!" she fumed.

No matter that it was Mr. Breezy who wrapped up the perfume of the fresh-cut grass and wildflowers along with the field lark's song and personally carried them down to the river's edge, just because he knew it would brighten the lives of the Misses Marsh—and even of hoity-toity Ms. Thing. No matter that it was he who, on summer days, fetched them a spell of cool relief from the stifling heat. No matter that it was he who, because he was out and about, brought them the latest news and tales of exciting, far-off lands.

Ms. Thing accepted Mr. Breezy's gifts as only her due. But to her way of thinking, he was a most inconvenient man. The fact that he showed up whenever the mood struck him and actually expected courtesy absolutely galled her. "A true gentleman never arrives unannounced," she admonished her cousins after one of Mr. Breezy's visits.

"Ah, but we do so love a man who is spontaneous!" replied the Marshes.

"You know what spontaneity leads to, don't you?" Ms. Thing asked in her most patronizing tone. The Marshes shook their heads. "Anarchy and ruin," she concluded triumphantly. "Anarchy and ruin!"

"Really?" said the Misses Marsh. "Who'd have thought it!" Of course, they didn't agree with a word Ms. Thing was saying, but they knew better than to try to argue with her when her mind was made up.

One day, Mr. Breezy paid a call on the ladies, but he wasn't in possession of either his typical, cheery humor or his usual gifts to them.

"No bird songs this afternoon, Mr. Breezy?" noted Ms. Thing disdainfully. "How like a man to disappoint."

"I'm sorry, Ms. Thing," he replied in earnest, "but I'm a trifle preoccupied." She only sniffed and tossed her leaves in a huffy way. Mr. Breezy continued, "Ms. Thing and Misses Marsh, I've just stopped by to warn you that my cousin, Doctor Storm, is headed into town. In fact, he's told me he's planning to come right this way."

"And why should that concern us?" Ms. Thing wanted to know.

"Now, you and the Misses Marsh know as well as I that Dr. Storm can be a bit overwhelming, especially, shall we say, when the spirit is upon him — which, I might add, it is."

"The doctor is quite a character," the Misses Marsh admitted, "but we have always quite enjoyed his visits . . . even if it does sometimes take us three days to get our hair back to behaving after he's gone."

"Well, I must be heading off," said Mr. Breezy, taking his leave.

Ms. Thing grumbled so deeply her roots quaked. "Bah," she said. "Doctor Storm indeed!" But Ms. Thing didn't have much time to stew in her sanctimonious juices, for all at once the sky turned nearly black and a great howling surge of air yanked at her branches.

"Ms. Thing, Doctor Storm is just over the hill!" cried the Misses Marsh. "We do so wish you'd try to be hospitable and agree to just one dance with him."

"Never," replied Ms. Thing adamantly. "I shall never step to that ruffian's tune. I shall not budge one inch, do you hear me?"

But the Misses Marsh could not hear her, for a clap of thunder and a bolt of lightning announced that Doctor Storm had arrived with the spirit upon him such as they had never seen before. The Misses Marsh bowed low, then gave themselves up to the dance. Doctor Storm whirled them and swirled them this way and that. And just when they thought he was ready to relinquish his embrace, he would take them for another spin until they were quite giddy and nearly exhausted with ecstasy.

For her part, Ms. Thing remained true to her word. Though her leaves were torn asunder and her branches cartwheeled like crazy windmills, she would not budge. The Misses Marsh, caught up as they were in the moment, lost track of her—until, that is, they heard that awful chorus, more awful than the thunder or the wind—the noise that came as the very core and roots of Ms. Thing were torn from the soil, the rending moan that split the day as her thick, majestic trunk snapped in two as if she were no weightier than a twig, and the final, terrific clap as she fell broken on the bank of the river, her proud limbs dragging in the muddy foam.

And all at once, as quickly as he'd come, Doctor Storm was gone again. The Misses Marsh, sodden and somewhat bedraggled, stood up to take in the sorry scene. "Oh, poor Ms. Thing," they lamented.

A few moments later, Mr. Breezy passed by and laid a solemn kiss on Ms. Thing's lifeless brow, gently caressed her torn, wretched leaves and before he left, wove one last bird song through her ruined branches.

● ● ●

The moral? You get the idea. No one is proposing that you should ever compromise your deeply held beliefs or personal boundaries, but by learning to tune in to the needs of others and bend a little, you'll have the chance to actually become a stronger, more resilient person.

The other benefit to admitting that you don't always have to be right is that, besides allowing you to extract that broomstick from your butt, it can also be tremendously liberating and enlightening. The more spiritual doors you open, the better chance joy and knowledge have of finding their way into your house.

8. Be spontaneous.

You don't have to plan out a rigid dating strategy to have a good time. If something unexpected gets tossed into the mix, it doesn't necessarily have to spoil things. When we learn to go with the flow and live in the moment, life can be a lot more fun.

Case in point: Janey had been going out with Kevin for only a few weeks, and things between them couldn't have been better. They'd spent their first date rollerblading and eating pizza; for their second meeting, it was brunch and a museum. The coming Friday night was supposed to be their first "big evening"—champagne, a fine meal, and dancing at an intimate jazz club afterward.

Janey was on Cloud Nine. She'd splurged on a new dress and had her nails done. But on Friday afternoon when Kevin called to let her know what time he'd be picking her up, she could tell that something in his tone was a shade off. Concerned, she asked him what was up.

Kevin confessed that his best friend Jerry had suddenly been called out of town on urgent business and had to give up tickets for two prime seats to an NBA playoff game that Kevin would give his right arm to see. The problem was, the tickets were for that night.

Now, Janey was no great basketball fan—in fact, she knew next to nothing about the game—but she could tell how much seeing his favorite team in the playoffs meant to Kevin. "Has Jerry given them to anyone else yet?" she asked him.

"No, but . . ."

"Then put me on hold and call him back," Janey said. "Tell him you'll take the tickets."

Thirty seconds later, he clicked back on the line. "I've got them," Kevin told her ecstatically.

"That's wonderful," Janey said. "What time does the game start?"

"Eight o'clock."

"If you pick me up at six, will we still have time to grab a bite to eat first?" she asked.

"Sure thing," he replied, somewhat taken aback. "Listen, Janey, I know we had a special night planned, and you must be really disappointed . . ."

"I'm not worried. We'll get to it," Janey told him, then added with a laugh, "Just don't try this on my birthday."

"No way," Kevin replied.

That night when he picked her up, Kevin was all smiles, and even though it turned out to be a hot dog and beer night instead of filet mignon and champagne, they both had a fantastic time. Kevin was more than a little impressed that Janey cared enough about what mattered to him to alter their plans. The next day, he sent her a dozen long-stemmed roses, and the following weekend, when their postponed "big date" finally took place, the night was pure magic.

What if Janey, knowing how much the game meant to Kevin, had stood firm and insisted that they proceed with the evening's plans? Wouldn't she have been teaching him a lesson in priorities—showing him that if he truly valued her, she was worth his sacrificing something he cared about to show her that he cared about her more? There are some who will tell you that this is exactly what she should have done, and there are actually some men who like women who treat them this way—but for most, it would leave a bad taste behind. Men do want the women they date to be special, but they also hope that women feel that they're special, too.

Now, some of you may be shaking your heads and saying that Janey was crazy to let Kevin get away with a stunt like that. If he had been any kind of a real man, he would have bagged the game, right? Well, Kevin had been prepared to do just that, but he couldn't pretend to Janey that the game wasn't important to him. By being honest, Kevin let Janey know that his hesitation didn't have anything to with her personally. Had they gone on with business as usual and Kevin had then found himself unable to keep his mind from straying to thoughts of what he was missing, you can bet there's a good chance that Janey would have internalized his behavior and blamed herself for having done something wrong. But, armed with the truth and the power to be flexible enough to field his unexpected pass and run with it, both of them were able to come out winners.

Relationships are organic things, constantly growing, shifting, changing. You have to be able to adapt your behavior to make sure they thrive. Say you brought home a cactus and cared for it as you would an orchid. Even though you would be killing it with kindness, the results would be the same—a dead cactus.

Different men, and different relationships, have differ-ent needs. And depending on where you are, you may find your own desires modified by the circumstances of your life. But if you only let yourself act and react by one script—and it's from *Hello, Dolly!*—you'll run the risk of severely limiting your opportunities for happiness, romantic and otherwise.

Is letting a man change plans at the last minute setting a bad precedent or opening the door to a string of broken promises? Only if you let it. In a good relationship, sometimes having your way will be really important, and sometimes he'll need to have his. The key is learning to balance the two and keep an open mind.

9. Be safe!

If your instincts are telling you that something or someone is truly dangerous, don't hesitate to walk away. It's great to be fearless, but foolish is something else entirely. Don't let people talk you into behavior that makes you uncomfortable. Don't allow them to manipulate you into doing things you know you're going to regret.

No one's radar is 100 percent accurate all the time, but if yours is telling you to steer clear of a guy, or to bail out of a dubious situation—just do it. Never allow your fear of being thought "uncool" or of having to spend your time alone override your real best interests.

"I'd met Bob at a party," Shannon recalls. "He was a lot of fun, but a little more over the top than my usual taste. I let him talk me into going back to his place, but on the way over, I began to feel uneasy. Suddenly, I knew I wanted to go home and I told him so. His response was fairly hostile. He said he'd take me, but he'd left his dog cooped up inside all day and he had to take him out for a walk first. We pulled up to his place and I told him I'd just stay in the car. 'Suit yourself,' he said.

"He walked in and left the door open behind him. I didn't hear anything, no dog, no nothing. After a few minutes, I started to get scared. I got out of the car and went to the door. There he was, sitting on the steps with his pants unzipped. 'C'mon, baby,' he leered. 'Wanna come inside and play with my doggie?'

"I just turned around and ran down the driveway into the street. I was practically hysterical. Fortunately, there was a bus stop on the corner and I just made one that was pulling out. I didn't care where I was going as long as it was away from there. It still makes my skin crawl just thinking about it! From that moment on, whenever my gut says 'No!' you'd better believe I trust it."

If a man mistreats you, hand him his walking papers, because after the first time, there should never be a second. The violence perpetrated by men who are physically and emotionally abusive almost always escalates.

"When we were first going out, Clark seemed almost perfect," D'Arcy says. "Sure there'd be times when he'd overreact to things and he'd lose his temper, but he never took his anger out on me, so I chose to overlook it.

"We were going to take our first vacation together, a road trip up the California coast to Big Sur, and we were both really excited. We'd been driving only a couple of hours when this other driver cut Clark off. The guy had a map out on his seat and was obviously lost. The whole thing was a mistake, an accident. But Clark couldn't let it go. He just got madder and madder. At first, I thought he was kidding, but when he sped up and cut the guy off, I knew he was serious.

"'Okay, you're even now,' I told him. But he wouldn't calm down. He let the guy get ahead of him and then he started to tailgate him really close. I pleaded with him to stop it, but he just told me to shut up. Then he pulled up alongside the guy and actually tried to run him off the road. I was terrified. I could see the guy pointing to the back seat of his car, waving his arms. He was yelling something I couldn't hear. Then I saw it—a baby in a car seat, wailing its little lungs out. Scared as I was, I knew I had to do something.

"I tell you, God must have been looking out for me that day because just then, we hit a patch of heavy traffic and everyone had to slow down. Clark had pulled in behind the guy again and I think he was going to try to ram him from the rear. We were in the far right lane, so before Clark had a chance to step on the gas, I yanked the wheel really hard and we swerved up onto the shoulder.

"The other driver pulled away and I lost sight of him. Instead of yelling at me like I expected, Clark was all apologies, but that was the end of the trip — and the romance. I made him turn around and take me home. As much as I liked him, I refused to ever date him again."

Don't fool yourself with the "just this once" or "what harm could it do" rationales. Pursuing an affair with a questionable man can have disastrous consequences. Never forget, the most valuable thing you have is you. Don't put yourself in jeopardy.

10. Everything in moderation.

In our instant gratification culture, we all have a tendency to want to see results yesterday, especially when it comes to filling our most basic human need — finding love. But if you approach your quest for it as if it were a fad diet or a crash exercise program, you'll only have yourself to blame if you don't get the results you're seeking. Enthusiasm is wonderful, overzealousness can be just plain hazardous to your health.

See if this scene is familiar: Over the course of five years, Lucy had put on twenty pounds. Came the new year, she resolved to lose them, so she joined a gym, bought herself a supply of liquid weight-loss diet formula, and set to work. After an orientation session with a trainer at the gym, Lucy was ready for her first workout session.

She looked down at the little card the instructor had given her. Week One: After warm-up, three sets of fifteen sit-ups, followed by three sets of leg-lifts, fifteen reps. *No problem*, Lucy thought, *I'll just double it . . .* and so she did. For everything written down on the card, Lucy upped the weights, the reps, and the number of sets. Still, she somehow managed to get through the workout—but the next morning, she was so stiff and sore, she could barely get out of bed, much less think of going back to the gym.

Well, at least I can do the diet, she told herself. She read the label carefully, then mixed up her morning's ration of goo. She was about to drink it down, when another thought occurred to her. She went to the cabinet, pulled down a jar, then poured exactly half of her "breakfast" into it and put the rest away in the refrigerator. At noon, she drank the second half, and for dinner she ate a "sensible meal" as the diet brochure recommended. Feeling light-headed but determined, she fell asleep.

On the second day, she followed the same procedure. The third morning, Lucy woke up dizzy with hunger, but after her morning ration—this time a full one—she managed to convince herself that her body just needed time to get in tune with the diet. Her body, however, had other ideas. The more she tried not to think about food, the more she found she couldn't help herself. By 11 A.M., she couldn't take it anymore. She ran down to the kitchen and ransacked the freezer, popping a half-dozen prefab-junk-food-but-oh-so-tasty burgers in the microwave and scarfing them down in rapid succession. And that was the end of Lucy's diet.

Opting for an all-or-nothing quick-fix approach to finding love is no more of an answer than fad diets are to weight loss. You've got to look at the bigger picture and potentially restructure a lifetime's worth of habits, gradually and sensibly, to achieve your goals, so:

- Go for what you want, but not if what you're after belongs to someone else (like a married man or your sister's boyfriend). They say, "All's fair in love and war," but too many of us use that kind of thinking as an excuse to behave in ways that are childish, selfish, and unkind.
- Follow the Golden Rule, but don't spend all your time trying to second-guess what others may or may not need. People will let you know what their boundaries are soon enough. All you have to do is respect them.
- Be honest, but not to the point of cruelty. You don't have to tell a date every little thing that's on your mind, especially if what you're thinking isn't very flattering. Discretion really is the better part of valor. You can end an evening by being direct, and still leave your date's ego intact. (That Golden Rule thing, again.)
- Be open, but not overbearing. If you're out on a date and something has upset you, or you're not feeling happy at a particular moment, there's nothing wrong with expressing those feelings. We all have a bad night and need a shoulder to cry on once in a while, and hopefully, the men we date will be up to it. However, no man wants to date a woman so self-centered that all she can talk about is herself, or to be constantly on call to minister to a gaping wound.
- Trust your common sense, but don't jump to conclusions too quickly. Even the best men go through bad times, and sometimes you have to cut them some slack. If a man isn't responding to you with as much enthusiasm as you'd hoped, it's possible that he's not interested, or is only out to get what he can from you. On the other hand, maybe he's just hit a rough patch in his life and can't concentrate on you the way he'd truly like to be able to. If you think this may be the case, try to take a step back. You may be giving him the space

he needs to come around, and yourself the distance you need to get a perspective on what the real deal is.

- Have reasonable expectations, but don't lower your standards. Just as you shouldn't look for a man who will transform your life, neither should you go out with every one of them who asks you. You can be dateless for a while and have no need to feel desperate. Take your time. Not all men are "keepers." Hell, not all of them are human. It's okay to be choosy and wait until a good one comes along.

- Be flexible, but don't give up your principles. If a man crosses the line, let him know it. If his behavior is unacceptable to you, then tell him. If a man always expects you to give in to his whims, whatever they may be, drop him.

- Be spontaneous, but don't take a vacation from common sense. If your new beau calls you up for a spur-of-the-moment trip to Vegas and you've got a big presentation for the board of directors coming up in two days, calling in sick is probably not the best idea. In "the best of all possible worlds," we'd have instant gratification all of the time, but in the real world, irresponsibility is not the key to long-term happiness.

- Be safe, but don't let fear rule your life. We live in scary times. There are a lot of nuts out there who are looking to do us harm. Do everything in your power to avoid putting yourself in dangerous situations, but don't try to lock yourself away in an ivory tower. The prisons we build for ourselves work both ways: They keep the evil out, but at the same time they don't let the good in.

As I've said before, you can't look at romance as if it's a cult you're joining or a top-secret combat strike you're taking part in. So, while I believe it will really benefit you to follow the basic principles of dating I describe in this chapter, they are not the Ten Commandments, nor are they meant as a substitute for using your own judgment. Take them to heart, but don't go nuts.

I can't stress strongly enough that becoming the person you want to be and finding the love you need is a process. You may never have all the answers, because, hopefully, life will continue to offer you new questions and new options. You don't have to know where you're going to end up on this adventure. You just need to know how to have a great ride along the way — and that means opening your eyes to joy, staying true to your heart, and keeping yourself safe and healthy along the way.

CHAPTER SIX

Our Own Worst Enemy

Question: Who is the person most likely to sabotage your happiness?
Answer: You.

AS SURPRISING AS IT may seem, many women have a remarkable capacity for being their own worst enemies when it comes to finding a soul mate. Some strand themselves in a loveless wasteland, crazily obsessing over men who cannot or will not return their feelings, allowing their own spirits to wither and die; some dive blindly into the whitewater rapids of emotionally unstable, abusive men and are swept away by a current they can neither navigate nor control; while others put themselves safely on the shelf where no harm can come to them, except the harm of being forgotten and left unfulfilled.

Too often, women give in to "the big terror." *Oh my God*, we worry, *what if I wind up* (an ominous-sounding minor chord on the organ here, please) . . . *alone*. As we try to ward off the ever-increasing dread, our behavior can become so off-kilter and counterproductive that the big terror turns into a self-fulfilling prophecy. In fact, there are women who have been so scarred from past experiences that they will no longer allow themselves to feel any attraction to a man, lest they end up being hurt once again. The story of Molly illustrates this overly protective behavior.

• • •

A long time ago, far away from here, there was once a girl called Molly, who lived in a far-off kingdom called Allegory. Molly was a rather plain girl, and though she was certainly pleasant enough to look at, there was little chance that—as had happened to her fortunate neighbor, Cinderella—a wandering prince would be so taken with her grace and beauty that he'd sweep her up out of the ashes and make her his queen.

To be fair, Molly didn't spend too much of her time in the ashes anyway. She was a talented weaver, and the beautiful cloth she made was among the most highly prized in the land. From dawn to dusk, day in and day out, Molly could be found at her loom, humming softly to herself, coaxing the warp and woof of her threads into gossamer fabrics so extraordinary that when a delegation of visiting Chinese silk weavers saw them, they took one look, packed up their bags, and went home in disgrace.

Word of Molly's wondrous handiwork soon spread to every corner of the countryside—including the castle, the court, and eventually, the king. It so happened that King Dragon was about to be married to Princess Larkin, daughter of the ruler of the neighboring realm.

The nuptials were only three weeks off, and though the royal tailors and seamstresses were still working at a fever-ish pace to complete the king's new suit of clothes, they expected to be finished with it well before the happy day. Princess Larkin's wedding dress, however, was another story. Though they tried and tried, the merchants who supplied the court were unable to find a fabric to match the beauty of the bride, and so, with little time left, the seamstresses had not even begun to make Larkin's dress.

Upon hearing of Molly's fabulous creations, King Dragon called for his horse and a small company of men

at arms and rode out to see whether the girl's work
could possibly live up to her reputation. When he
arrived in the neighborhood where Molly lived, a whisper shot through the town like a bolt of lightning. There
could be only one reason the king stood at the threshold
of Molly's cottage, his gloved hand poised to knock
upon her door.

Tap, tap, tap went the king's knuckles with three
rapid-fire flicks of his wrist. Inside the cottage, the humming ceased. "I'll be right there," called Molly. When she
opened the door, she couldn't have been more flabbergasted. "Your Majesty," she said, dropping into the best
curtsy she could muster, hindered as she was by the
knocking of her knees, "you do me great honor by visiting my humble home. How may I be of service?"

"I have heard," said the king, "that you are the finest
weaver in my kingdom. I am looking for some cloth worthy to grace the beloved figure of my queen-to-be. As yet,
her wedding dress rests unmade, for though we have
searched the trade routes of the world, no one has found a
fabric equal to the undertaking. You may be my last hope."

Molly smiled. "Please, Your Majesty, step this way. I
think I may have just the thing."

King Dragon followed her to a tall cabinet that stood
at the back of the cottage. Gently and with tender care,
Molly removed a tissue-wrapped package from the shelf
and placed it on the table. Untying the silken ribbon that
bound it, she pulled back the paper to reveal the most
gorgeous piece of cloth the king—or anyone else—had
ever beheld. Its delicate, gossamer threads looked as if
they were woven out of midnight snow and candlelight.
The king held his breath and, reaching out with utmost
caution, grasped just the smallest corner and rubbed the
fabric, soft as an angel's wing, between his fingers.

"It's perfect," he told Molly.

"If it pleases you, then take it with my compliments," she replied.

King Dragon was a generous man. He reached down to his belt, pulled out a pouch of golden coins, and offered them to her as payment.

"No, Your Majesty," said Molly, "I cannot take your money. This was made for my own bridal gown, but that wedding is no longer to be. Since I have no wish to make profit from sorrow, I give the fabric to you as a gift. I hope it brings happiness to you and your bride."

"Thank you, mistress," answered the king, as he took up the treasure in his arms. "I will find a way to repay your kindness yet." Once outside her door, King Dragon sent one of his men-at-arms to look into the circumstances of Molly's distress.

"It's not a tale that hasn't been told a thousand times before," a neighbor informed the king's man. "She loved one who loved another better. It happens, but she is so afraid of ever being hurt again, she rarely ventures out of her cottage." When the soldier repeated the facts as he had heard them, King Dragon shook his head. *Perhaps Larkin can come up with some fitting compensation for the girl*, he thought to himself as he mounted his horse.

And so the king told his bride-to-be Molly's story, and how, because of her loss, she would take no payment for her wares. "I think it is bad luck not to give her something for her trouble though," the king mused.

"I have an idea," said Larkin. "Why not send Lunari to her and let him grant her her one dearest wish? I want this woman to be of good cheer on our wedding day."

Now, Lunari was the court magician, and a very powerful sorcerer. One did not seek his favors lightly. King Dragon thought for a moment about what Larkin had proposed, then nodded his head in assent. "Very well, my dearest," he replied, taking Larkin's hand. "You are as

generous and wise as you are beautiful." But even before
the last words had formed on his lips, the air was filled
by a strange cloud, and there before them stood Lunari.

"You have need of me, sire?" the magician asked,
though it was merely a courtesy. "What is your will?" So
King Dragon again recounted Molly's tale, then told
Lunari of Larkin's request.

"It shall be so," he answered, bowing low, and in the
blink of an eye, he was gone to do her bidding.

Molly, hearing a noise, stood up from the loom at
which she had been working steadily for many hours and
looked behind her. "Allow me to introduce myself," said
her unexpected guest. "I am the court magician, Lunari."
He then proceeded to tell Molly of Princess Larkin's
heartfelt gratitude, and explained that he had been
charged by her to grant Molly the one wish that spoke to
her innermost yearning. "Name the thing, and it shall be
yours," he told her.

Molly sat back down on the bench. She knew the
thing she wanted most—now she must find the words to
tell Lunari. She sat in silence for a few moments, and
when finally she spoke, this is what she said: "Three sum-
mers ago I loved a man, and I thought that he loved me,
but for all my wishing, I could never make it so."

"And is that what you want now, my dear?" Lunari
asked, gently laying his hand upon her shoulder.

"That man has a family now," she answered. "Should
I ask you to unmake all of that for my sake?"

"It is within my power to do so," Lunari told her.

"But that is not my wish," Molly said.

"Then tell me your true wish."

"When that man broke with me, it was as if my heart
had been torn from my chest by a cruel, unseen hand. For
the months that followed, I could neither sleep nor eat
nor work," she explained. "And though I lived, there was

many a night I wished that my body had died along with the love I'd squandered. After much time, eventually I came back to myself again, and yet, I know I can never come all the way back."

"Do you wish me to unmake that time?" Lunari asked her. "As a weaver, you must be aware that to pull a fabric apart and make it over is much more complex than to create something new."

"I would not be so bold as to ask such a great favor," Molly told him. "All I want is never to be hurt that way again. Can your magic make it so?"

"Why, yes, my dear," he assured her solemnly, "it can. If you're sure that is what you truly desire."

"That is my wish," Molly declared.

"Very well," said Lunari, stepping back a pace. Then, he closed his eyes, raised his hands, and knitted them through the air, blue sparks flying from his fingertips. An instant later, he bowed to Molly and vanished.

"How odd I feel," she said aloud, but she couldn't put her finger on what this sensation might be. It was neither good nor bad . . . only different. "Oh, well, it will sort itself out." Molly resumed her work, weaving until the sun's last rays fled her cottage window. When she finally stood up late that night to go to bed, Molly discovered a small crystal sphere sitting among the spools of thread on her workbench. When Molly picked it up, it warmed to her touch and felt strangely familiar, but she could not say why. She examined it closely and saw that there was a drop of something deep and crimson in its very core.

Of course she remembered nothing of Lunari's visit, for he had seen to that. But now, embedded like a living thing trapped in amber, lay that special key that unlocks the heart and welcomes love across its threshold. The magician had kept his word. He'd made Molly invulnerable to pain, but in so doing, he had also rendered her impervious to love.

For the rest of her life, Molly continued to weave her glorious goods. She never again loved, nor was she loved by a man, but it did not occur to her that something was amiss, though often when her day's work was behind her, she would sit by her fire, worrying the globe of glass in the palm of her hand, thinking that there was something she ought to be remembering. Then one night, many years later, when the son of the son of Dragon and Larkin ruled the land, she dozed off, letting the crystal tumble from her grip and fall into the embers. "Now I shall have to wait until morning to get it back," she fretted when she awakened, "if it isn't ruined."

"Allow me," a voice from out of the darkness offered. It was Lunari. He bent down, reached his hand into the burning coals, and retrieved the talisman.

All at once, Molly's wintry eyes grew bright. "I remember you," she told him.

"It's nearly time," Lunari warned.

"Is it?" Molly answered.

"I believe this belongs to you," Lunari stated, handing the crystal sphere to Molly. It melted at her touch. She heard a small sound, like a key turning in a rusty lock. And then a strange thing happened. In Molly's head, a vision unfolded like an endless tapestry, and woven into it were all the scenes of love and joy and sorrow that she might have known had she never made that one wish.

"Oh," said Molly with a sigh. "Oh . . ." And then she was gone.

• • •

Dropping out so they won't lose is just one way women undermine themselves in the race toward love.

So many are afraid of rejection and hurt that they'll do anything they can to prevent it, either by running away, as we've already discussed, or "getting to it before it gets to them." They try too hard, or they don't try at all. They leap headlong into the tiger's cage, or they don't even bother going to see the circus when it comes to town. They circumscribe their worlds with neat little boundaries, or they let the globe flatten them like a giant wrecking ball. Whatever the particular defense mechanism they choose to employ, each one keeps them from finding the love they desire and the fulfillment they deserve.

Women who let fear rule them have an uncanny knack for building barriers to their own happiness, often without even knowing they're doing it. They'll sit timidly at a broken red traffic signal of their own making, waiting for the light to change, never getting where they'd like to go, while everyone else on the road ends up navigating around them. While the green bulb may be in their own glove compartment all along, they may feel powerless to climb up the light pole and screw it in.

In a case like this, sometimes it's better to risk getting the ticket. If an old habit is holding you back, instead of trying to dismantle it all at once, go around it. Now, I don't mean that you should throw caution to the wind and go speeding blindly through the intersection. In love and driving, you must always look both ways and check your blind spots before going forward. However, to quote a great statesman, "We have nothing to fear but fear itself." So take a deep breath, take your foot off the brake, check your rearview mirror, and remember that you must . . .

- **Try and Try Again**

You know that old cliché, "Nothing ventured, nothing gained"? It's the truth. If you spend your life hiding from love, it probably won't find you. You've got to put yourself out there to get what you want. It may not happen as quickly as you'd like, and that can be pretty scary, but if you don't make the effort, you have only yourself to blame for the consequences.

- **Think for Yourself**

Like the chronic get-rich-quick schemer who tries out every new money-making gimmick that comes down the pike, each one promising to be the be-all, end-all, and once-and-for-all answer, when it comes to love, many women persist in putting blind faith in the advice of others in trying to achieve their own romantic ends, not realizing there's a big catch involved. To hand over your right to make your own decisions is to give up your freedom of choice. Is that what you really want? What makes someone else's beliefs more valid than your own? They're not.

Of course, there are those who use convention as a crutch—the "I did everything *they* said and it didn't work out, so it can't be *my* fault" crowd. These folks may think they're trying everything they can to succeed, but in reality, they're just hiding from themselves and from the truth. Love fads are like diet fads. They don't work. You have to look at the overall pattern of your behavior, determine what's preventing you from getting what you want, then work on making a change within yourself to bring about the desired result.

- **Accept Failure**

When they find love, many people convince themselves, *This is it!* Then, when they lose it, they think, *I can never be happy again!* But it doesn't work that way. Don't cheat yourself by believing that your existence is laid out like some big jigsaw puzzle in which only one piece will ever fit perfectly into the slot of love. Life is really a lot more like a collage—there are many possible things you can toss into the mix and still come up with something that's a real work of art. If the first thing you try, or even the second or third, turns out not to be the right match, it's not the end of the world. As painful as losing love might be, when you close one door, another one opens. (I hate it when my mother is right.) I'm not going to try to dispute the fact that rejection sucks. It does. Big time. But you can get over it, and it really *is* better to have loved and lost than never to have loved at all.

- ### Know When to Abandon Ship

  If you find yourself in a situation that isn't working out, there's no law that says you have to stay in it. Nothing is etched in stone. If you've made a mistake, it's all right to move on. Yes, you might hurt someone's feelings, but in the long run, staying somewhere you're miserable is unhealthy for both partners. This is not to say that you should bolt at the first sign of trouble. Every relationship hits bumps—even big, nasty ones. But if in your heart of hearts, you know that what you're in can never be right, you have to be able to give yourself permission to walk away.

- ### Treat Men Fairly

  Sure it's okay to flirt. It's fine to date on a casual basis. What *isn't* fine is to string a guy along just so you can have someone to spend Saturday nights with until "a good one" comes your way.

  If you find that after a few dates, a guy you're not sure about is heading toward a much more serious commitment than you're ready to make, again, honesty is really the best policy. There are ways to let a man know that you're undecided without shooting him out of the air.

However, if you've already figured out that there's no real potential for the two of you, you owe it to the guy to toss him back into the big pond. And do it gently.

If you do see potential, don't presume to know what's on his mind. The males of our species are not all like Pavlov's dogs, drooling on cue when given the proper stimulus. Men are thinking, feeling beings — okay, maybe not all of them, all of the time — who deserve to be credited for their intelligence. (This is why anyone who tells you that a man will never leave you if you use the right bait is just plain crazy. Contrary to popular opinion, men aren't trained seals in a pond who jump just because you toss them a nice fish. There are plenty of nice fish out there, and plenty of women tossing them.)

• Control Your Own Life, Not His

For eons, women have had to put up with that "I know what's best for you, dear" paternalistic poppycock, and did we like it? Hell, no! So why expect your lover to roll over and show you his belly when you treat him in a similar fashion? There are few things in life more aggravating than someone who decides that they know what's best for you, better than you know it yourself.

Some might say, "Well, *we* had to put up with it, so should they! We want equal time, dammit!" If that's how you feel, you're letting anger cloud your judgment. Face it. This was a pretty bogus proposition from the minute it first reared its ugly head. It's time to let it crawl back under the rock from whence it came and move on. Romance isn't about getting a man to tango to your tune, it's about finding a rhythm you *both* can dance to together, because synchronicity is where the real magic is.

If you do feel the need to run someone's life and you find yourself consistently gravitating toward men who have to be "organized for their own good," you might want to ask yourself why. There's a good chance that there's something in your own past that you may not be looking at, and that that is what's really in need of fixing. Maybe when you were growing up, your parents weren't around too much and the role of caregiver fell to you. Perhaps you lived in an environment where you almost always got your way. Or possibly you came from a family living in chaos, and imposing control on yourself and those around you was your way of dealing with it.

Whatever the cause, if you're still acting out this pattern as an adult, it's something you should probably check into. Because chances are, if you find yourself repeatedly in pursuit of men whose lives are a big mess, it's more than likely that you're only using this maneuver to distract yourself from the real issues. Sure, it's a helluva lot easier to clean the skeletons out of somebody else's closet than to face up to looking in your own, but if you can find the courage to lay those bones to rest, you'll find that you no longer feel threatened by someone with his own needs and ways of doing things. Who knows? Maybe your way *is* better, but it could be that his way flies the kite, too.

• **Stick Up for Yourself**

If your potential lover is one of those men who must always be in control of their own actions and of those around them, it won't matter how flexible you are, you're going to wind up right where he wants you—under his feet. Not only is it okay for you to have opinions, it's paramount for you to express them. You're thinking, *But men won't like me if I'm too aggressive.* Well, you're right—nobody likes anybody who is. However, knowing your mind and stating what's on it don't have anything to do with being pushy, and a man—or someone like your mother, your aunt, or your best girlfriend—who tries to

con you into believing that it does, whatever their moti-
vation, is doing you more harm than good.

As women, many of us are taught that it's imperative
to please everyone as best we can—everyone, that is,
except ourselves. If yours is a personality that finds true
happiness in doing nice things for others, that's wonderful, but if constantly performing favors and giving gifts
of substance and self has become your way of ensuring
that you'll be appreciated, you aren't doing yourself any
service.

There's no earthly reason to put your own needs last.
True love is a balance. No one gets their way all the time.
Not him and not you. Yes, it's all right to compromise now
and then, but if you find that you're the one who's always
bending over backwards to be accommodating, you're
going to wind up with a permanent pain in the neck. My
advice is to stand up straight. I guarantee that not only will
the caliber of your relationships improve, but you'll see the
world from a much better perspective, as well.

We human beings often get into the worst trouble
when we try to think for others. Hell, it's hard enough
thinking for ourselves most of the time. The kind of logic
that says "Since I've done *A*, then he must feel *B*" would
be fine if having a relationship were an exact science like
math, but it's not. If you allow yourself to fall into the
trap of second-guessing your lover's intentions, you may
be in for some major headaches—not to mention
heartaches, to boot.

• **Take All the Time You Need**

Think of the pickup techniques that have succeeded
with you in the past. Guys who come on as strong as three-
dollar cologne make you gag, right? Well, that works both
ways. There's nothing wrong with approaching a man, but
if every time you meet "a keeper," your eyes light up like a

creature of the damned and your nails morph into grappling hooks, it's a good bet that you won't be keeping him for very long.

You don't have to be a rocket scientist to know that driving a car fifty miles per hour over the speed limit can lead to disaster, but on the road to love, a lot of women recklessly put the pedal to the metal, setting themselves up for the big crash and burn—and it doesn't have to happen. It's great to be excited, to be in the moment, to ask for what you want—but you've got to let things follow their natural course and give them the time they need to grow at their own pace. If you do, you may actually get where you want to go *and* enjoy the ride along the way. Which leads us to the mother of all dating faux pas—desperation, or "The Big D."

The truth is, when it comes to desperation, guys have radar that's singularly sensitive. A man can usually detect an overzealous female from a block away. As frightened as some women are about how and when they're ever going to find that perfect relationship, they can become even more frightening to the very men they're seeking out. Each likely guy—and some not-so-likely guys—who crosses their path might possibly be "the one who is going to save me." And before the poor bastard can say "Jack Rabbit," he's suddenly saddled with the burden of being the knight in shining armor—when most of the time, all he was looking for was maybe a casual date and some good conversation over a beer or two.

Eventually, these self-defeating patterns can become so familiar they're almost comforting. Our worst habits are transformed into trusted companions; our most dire excuses sometimes become our dearest friends. We repeat the same mistakes time and time again, swearing that each time will be the last, but knowing somewhere deep inside that it isn't the case. And so it was with Emily.

• • •

Emily was a loving, bright, and giving girl. She was funny, creative, attractive, and not lacking in social graces. She also wanted to get married and have a family. She wanted this so much, in fact, that it became somewhat of an obsession. In her quest to find the perfect mate, she began to see every man as potentially perfect. Every time the new "Mr. Right" came along, Emily would pounce on him and do everything she could to plug him in to her family scenario. When these liaisons inevitably ended — usually almost before they'd even begun — she often couldn't understand why.

One day, during a conversation with her college roommate Amanda, who had since moved halfway across the country, Emily was again bemoaning the dearth of datable men. Amanda, whose own ten-year marriage was currently on shaky ground, could only sympathize.

"I'm going to wind up a demented old bag lady feeding pigeons in Central Park," Emily declared.

"If things keep going the way they have been," Amanda replied with a sigh, "maybe I'll join you."

"It's too bad we don't know anyone we could fix each other up with," Emily remarked.

"Wait a minute," Amanda said. "I've got the perfect guy for you. He's charming, he's funny, and he's smart as a whip."

"He's the dog-faced boy, right?" Emily asked with a laugh.

"No way," Amanda replied. "In fact, you've told me on more than one occasion that you thought he was extremely attractive and very sexy."

"And just who might this paragon of virtue be?" Emily wanted to know.

"My brother, Marty!" Amanda chirped.

"Your brother Marty is married and living in Tucson," Emily pointed out.

"Correction," said Amanda. "My brother Marty is divorced and moving to New York next week and he doesn't know a soul! Shall I give him your number and have him call you?"

"Well," Emily answered, trying to keep the rising excitement that had suddenly taken hold of her out of her voice, "I guess that would be all right."

"Good!" said Amanda, and true to her word, that is exactly what she did.

A few nights later, Marty called to reintroduce himself to Emily. They talked for hours, laughing and reminiscing over old times. Marty was coming to town in a few days. They made plans to meet the following Saturday afternoon at the skating rink in Rockefeller Center. "I hope you remember what I look like," said Emily as their conversation drew to a close. "It's been a while."

"Of course I remember," Marty assured her. "No one could forget a knockout like you."

Emily had already named their children by the time she'd hung up the phone. She could hardly wait to call up her mom to tell her to take the antique lace wedding dress she'd been saving out of mothballs. *Hmm, I wonder what kind of music Marty likes?* she found herself musing over her coffee and health muffin the next morning. *Maybe that great jazz quartet that played at our office Christmas party would be available for the reception . . .*

On Saturday, Marty met her with a bouquet of tulips and a warm hug. They rented skates and spent a splendid hour on the ice. Marty was an excellent skater, and though Emily was a little rusty, she managed to hold her own. But each time Marty's hand reached to the small of her back to guide her through a turn, Emily felt a little quiver run through her that had nothing to do with the frigid weather.

After the skating session, they decided to head downtown to an intimate little restaurant that had been Emily and Amanda's favorite in their college days. Marty and Emily waited at the bar until a cozy table by the fireplace became vacant. As the evening progressed, their attraction for one another grew. Marty was even more handsome than Emily had remembered. His personality was a combination of a warm, friendly manner mixed with a wry, insightful humor that she found intoxicating.

By the time dessert arrived, Marty had begun the story of his past marriage and what went wrong. Emily listened sympathetically as Marty unraveled the tale of his failed marriage, wondering how anyone could let someone this special get away. The bottom line, he said, was that they'd married too young and had grown apart. They wanted different things. He was ready for a family. His wife was totally focused on her career. There were no hard feelings; in fact, he and his ex were still friends, but it had been time to move on.

Inside, Emily was nearly crowing with delight. *He wants kids! He wants to get married again! He's perfect!* She told Marty that while she loved her career, she too was thinking a lot about having a baby these days. "That old biological clock is beginning to sound more and more like Big Ben," she quipped, then found herself confessing, "What I'd really like to do is just take a few years off and do the mommy thing full-time . . . but I'll have to find the right man first, of course." At that point, the check came, and though Emily offered to split it, Marty insisted on paying.

By then, it was fairly late. The chill winds blowing off the Hudson buffeted them together as they walked toward the parking garage where Marty had left his car.

Marty gave his parking stub to the attendant, who disappeared into the catacombs. Emily put her hands into the pockets of Marty's overcoat and pulled him close. "Come home with me," she said, kissing him with rising passion.

"Are you sure?" he asked.

"More than sure," she replied. Emily spent the drive home in a blissful fog, her hand gently resting midway on Marty's upper thigh. They barely made it through her apartment door before ripping each other's clothes off.

The next morning, Marty's demeanor was affectionate but slightly distant. "I really should be getting home," he told Emily as he dressed. "I've got to pack."

"Pack? But I thought you hadn't even unpacked yet."

"I haven't," he said, bending over to give her a kiss on the forehead, "but I have to go to a sales conference in Denver. It starts tomorrow morning, so I'll be flying out this afternoon."

"Oh," Emily responded, unable to hide her disappointment. "I see."

"Tell you what," Marty said, "I'm back Friday. What do you say we hop in the car, then go for a ride and spend the weekend someplace romantic?"

"That sounds wonderful," Emily declared, her mood brightening immediately.

"Great," said Marty as he grabbed his things. "I'll call you around the middle of the week and we'll figure something out."

Emily was so happy she was practically floating two feet off the ground. After Marty left, she got dressed and took a walk around her neighborhood. As she was passing a bookstore, she happened to see a beautifully illustrated hardbound edition of Shakespeare's sonnets. Without a moment's hesitation, she went in and, though the price was high, bought it. *While I'm out*, she thought to herself, *I should pick up a few things for Marty's apartment . . . and judging from what he wore the other night, he hasn't got nearly enough warm clothes for this weather. I should probably take care of that, too.*

Two sweaters, half a dozen pairs of thermal socks, four coffee mugs, a spice rack, a few dish towels, and an alarm clock that sported the Tasmanian Devil on its face later, Emily made her way home, well pleased. She took the price tags off the merchandise and made them into a sort of "care package," except for the book, which she opened and inscribed, *"To Marty, the answer to my prayers. All my love, Emily."*

That done, she spent the rest of the day figuring out what she was going to bring the following weekend. Outfits were tried on and rejected. She retrieved her "good" lingerie from its tissue-lined box and packed it into her overnight bag along with the travel kit that contained her toiletries, makeup, and the new box of special condoms she'd purchased for the trip. Next, she went to her CD collection and picked out some good driving music, plus something more romantic, should they decide to pull off to the side of the road somewhere. She'd even remembered to pick up trail mix and bottled water.

Saturday dawned, and Emily was up with the sun, as eager as a child on Christmas morning. Her overnight case already stood like a sentinel by her door, next to the bag that held the CDs and road supplies she'd packed. She couldn't wait to catch the look on Marty's face when he saw the things she'd gotten for him.

At a few minutes past ten, the doorbell rang. It was Marty. She gave him a big kiss, then took him by the hand and led him to the living room. "I've got a surprise for you," she said, barely able to contain her excitement.

"It looks like you've been busy," he answered, sizing up the abundant care package that overflowed onto the coffee table. "This stuff is great, but you really shouldn't have."

"Wait, there's one more thing," she told him, grabbing the volume of Shakespeare off the side table and handing it to him with a big smile.

"Emily, you're too much."

"Read the inscription," she directed.

"Thanks, Emily," he told her after he'd read it, "but like I said, you really shouldn't have. I guess we should get going."

Marty and Emily piled all the gear in his car and headed toward the Pocono resort at which he'd made reservations. From time to time he'd fuss with the radio or ask Emily if she needed to stop for anything, but for the most part, he was silent. And soon Emily, exhausted from her daybreak wake-up call, allowed herself to fall asleep.

When they checked into the hotel, Marty took off his shoes and lay down on the bed. Emily climbed in next to him and nuzzled herself in close, nibbling on his earlobe and running her hand suggestively along his thigh. Marty rolled away from her, picked up the TV remote from the nightstand, and handed it to her. "I've got to catch a few Zs," he said. "Why don't you watch a movie? It won't bother me."

"All right," Emily answered, feeling a sudden pang of misgiving, "I guess that's okay."

"Sorry, kid, I'm bushed. Wake me up around six and we'll go have a nice dinner and see the show."

Though Emily was beginning to suspect that something was wrong, she shooed the thought out of her head. *He's just tired,* she told herself as she watched him sleep. At six, she woke him clad in nothing but a towel. "Care to join me in the shower?" she asked mischievously.

"No, thanks," he answered. "I'm funny about bathroom things. I like my privacy."

"Okay, then. I'll just be a minute."

"Take your time," he told her, picking up the remote. "I want to check the basketball scores on the news."

During dinner, Marty seemed to get back to his former charming self. They enjoyed a lovely meal and some great conversation, then headed to the lounge to take in the stand-up comedy bill that the hotel had booked.

At the end of the evening, Marty and Emily headed back to their room, and this time, it was Marty who began the seduction. This time the sex was only so-so, but Emily wrote it off to too much alcohol and felt reassured that Marty truly cared for her.

The next morning was uneventful and by the early afternoon, they were headed back to the city. Emily dutifully popped the CDs she'd brought into the player while Marty drove. The sun was just going down when Marty pulled the car up in front of Emily's apartment. "Aren't you coming in?" she asked as she grabbed her bag off the back seat.

"No," he told her, "I've got to get some paperwork together for a presentation tomorrow. I'll call you later."

After a couple of days, when Marty still hadn't phoned, she called him, only to get his answering machine. She left a message, then called back an hour later and left another. The same thing happened the next night and the one after. *Maybe he had to go out of town unexpectedly*, she told herself, trying not to panic. *He travels so much . . .*

The next evening when she returned home from work, the light on her machine was blinking. The message was from Marty, all right, but it wasn't the one she was expecting. "Emily, I know this is really lame," he began, "but I don't think we should see each other anymore. You're a great girl and you deserve the best, but . . . well, it's just not working for me. I'm sorry."

The next night when the phone rang, Emily's heart leapt. *He's changed his mind*, she hoped wildly. But when she picked up the phone it wasn't Marty, it was Amanda.

"I heard things didn't go so well with you and Marty," she said. "I just wanted to check up to see if you're all right."

"Not really," Emily confessed. "I just don't understand what happened. I thought he really liked me."

"He does like you, Emily, but . . ."

"But what? Tell me, Amanda. What?"

"You scared him. He said every time you looked at him, it was like you saw a tattoo on his forehead that read 'Future father of my children,' " Amanda explained.

"But he told me he *wants* kids. He *wants* to get married," Emily countered miserably.

"He does, honey," Amanda said soothingly. "But a relationship isn't like instant oatmeal. You can't just add boiling water and thirty seconds later expect that it's all set. I'm sorry, Emily, but it's the truth. You've got to be in love with the person, not the *idea* of the person or the idea of being married."

• • •

If you're in the habit of going overboard with relationships—especially when they're new—it's important that you not kid yourself into believing that all the thinking and planning and "doing" you're frantically involved in and obsessing over is about satisfying the needs of your lover. What's really happening is that you've allowed your own hunger to be part of a twosome to become so demanding that it's sucking you in and swallowing you up. If you can learn to recognize this "black hole" for what it is, instead of trying to fill it—which is impossible—you'll be able to avoid it.

The Fine Arts of Flirting and Dating

NOW THAT WE'VE TAKEN a look at the field and at the underlying principles of the mating game, it's time to learn some warm-up techniques, some strategy, and a few basic plays that will ensure that your next romantic liaisons will be winners. What do I mean by "winners"? Am I suggesting there's a magic formula that will transform you from a wallflower to a tiger lily? A simple equation in which adding A to B equals Finding Mr. Right? No!

In a winning relationship, you feel good about yourself and the other person; there's a positive flow of communication, plus a healthy helping of mutual respect. And while these are the qualities that can *potentially* lead to trust, love, and eventually commitment, they are no guarantee that every relationship you embark on will be "the one," no matter how much you'd like it to be or how much effort you put into making it so. However, if you do study these methods and apply them to your dating game plan, there's every possibility that you will meet lots of great men, enjoy their company, and enhance your self-esteem in the process.

The Warm-Up

Before you begin any serious endeavor, it's a good idea to prep yourself first. So even though you've studied for that important test, or built up your stamina for the big race, you've still got to do the warm-up exercises that will loosen you up, clear your mind of anxieties, and get you ready to participate in the main event. Here are three things to try before you hit the field:

Enjoy the day.

This is not something that you actively "do" to seek out a man, it's more a matter of putting yourself in a state of mind that will create an aura of attraction around you. If you're having fun, people will want to be near you. It's that simple. No one is happy all the time, nor should they be, but even in your worst moments, if you can find one small thing that gives you pleasure, it can do a lot more for you than just alter your mood.

"I was having the mother of all days," reports Kim, a twenty-two-year-old personal assistant. "Everything was going wrong. It was raining and there had been a water main break near my apartment building, which meant not only no hot water, but a forty-five-minute delay added to my commute. When I got to work, I was drenched and my boss was screaming for a report he couldn't find—which we later found buried on his desk—plus I snagged my last pair of pantyhose on the copier. By noon, I felt like I'd gone ten rounds with Evander Holyfield.

"On my lunch hour, I decided to go out and get some new pantyhose. The rain had stopped. Just as I was crossing the street, the sun came out. There was a big puddle and on top of it was this floating rainbow—I guess from gasoline or something—but the colors were so beautiful and shimmery, I couldn't help but smile. Then I saw that there was a man's face reflected in the puddle and he was smiling, too. I looked up and realized that even though we'd shared only this one tiny, magical thing, it was kind of a bond between us.

"Maybe it was silly. I don't know, but I just suddenly felt light. Free. And I was still smiling when he asked me to lunch. . ."

Put yourself out there!

Now, as simple as that sounds, there are still many gals out there laboring under the false impression that love will come to you, you don't have to go to it. But if you're sitting at home, or simply shuttling back and forth from your office to your apartment, odds are love is not going to find you. Sure there's the off chance that you might fall for your cable installer, plumber, or mailman, but as a general rule, love does not make house calls. You have to make an effort!

You're thinking *Singles bars? Gag! No way!* Right? Well, there are plenty of places to meet men that aren't singles bars, although, as bad a reputation as they might have, they are still great venues to *practice* in. Just remember: You don't have to consume alcohol to make yourself brave. You can sit at one of these places sipping club soda and get the same results if you put your mind to it.

On the other hand, if you just can't bring yourself to cross the threshold of your local Fern & Brew, here are a few alternatives: There's a new breed of indoor sports complexes that offer amenities like wall climbing, driving ranges, racquetball and handball courts, simulated skiing, and enough other activities to boggle the imagination. Got a dog? Take him to a park or the beach instead of the usual trot around the block. Try bowling alleys. Really. They're "retro-cool" right now; just try to avoid "league nights." Then there are coffee house/bookstores (yes, they're cliché, but again, still feasible places to break yourself in); museums (especially good for singles with kids); concerts; sporting events; supermarkets . . . use your imagination. The trick to this is finding the places you'd likely have a good time at anyway, and putting yourself in a frame of mind that says, *I'm going to enjoy myself, whether I meet a man or not*.

It's silly to go someplace you wouldn't normally visit in a million years. For example, trotting off to a lumberyard and coming home with a pile of useless two-by-fours just because there was a cute guy there to help you load them into your car may not be the best idea. Do museums bore you to tears? Avoid them. If you're a monster truck rally kind of gal, go for it! Wherever you go, just have fun.

Squeeze out the sponge.

Many of us don't realize it, but we walk around carrying an entire day's, week's, or even lifetime's worth of negative energy with us everywhere we go. Without even knowing it, our fists are clenched, out eyes glare, and our lips curl into a snarl like Elvis's when he was told they were out of mayo.

The human psyche is like a sponge—once it's full, especially of things like anger and frustration, it can't absorb anything else. Even the good things like love. In order to be receptive to new experiences and new emotions, we've got to squeeze out the sponge from time to time. Do whatever it takes. Meditate. Read a book. Play racquetball or work out at the gym. Take yourself out to a movie or rent an old favorite. Treat yourself to a hot bath or an extra hour's sleep on Sunday morning.

Find the thing that releases your stress and then give yourself permission to let your problems go for a little while—they'll still be there when you get back to them. But hopefully, you'll have a new perspective on dealing with them that won't take up the whole sponge.

Three Things Men Know That Women Should Learn

Just as there is no one pickup line or technique that works on every woman, there's no one surefire method to catch the fancy of every man. It's a shame that each one doesn't come with his own individual *How to Win My Affections* manual. However, there are certain standard operating procedures that hold true for pretty much every make and model, and so this section will offer a few suggestions to get you started.

Now, some may tell you that when it comes to the art of getting yourself noticed by members of the opposite sex, men and women are wired up to totally different motherboards, and that what works for the Martians doesn't fly for the Venusians. Historically speaking, however, men have had a lot more practice at being the choosers than the choosees, and as much as we women might be loath to admit it, we can apply the lessons they've learned over the centuries to our own search for love—or perhaps we should say lovers.

There are certain behavior traits traditionally associated with male energy and female energy, or what Asian cultures call yin and yang. By adapting a few of the yin principles for yang use, women can find new ways to achieve self-confidence and success when establishing first contact with would-be romantic interests.

1. Ask out a hundred—date five.

This tactic is all about percentages. If you haven't been dating for a while, it's also a great way for you to get your feet wet and practice your pickup skills. It's something that Cindy, a self-described "Olympic Dater," learned "a million years ago" from a guy she knew in high school named Chuck.

"Chuck was a babe-magnet," Cindy recalls. "There wasn't a Saturday night that went by when he didn't have a date. He went out with lots of different girls, all pretty, all nice. You never knew who he was going to show up with. Part of his appeal had to do with the fact that he was a jock who played on the football team and the baseball team—of course, the fact that he had a great smile and killer dimples didn't hurt, either.

"One afternoon, Chuck was hanging out with my brother, who was also on the football and baseball teams. They were shooting some baskets when the subject of girls came up. I was sitting nearby on the porch, carving a twig with my not-very-sharp pocket knife, but since I was a younger sibling, and a little sister to boot, I might as well have been invisible.

"'All right,' my brother asked, 'how do you do it? You've got girls practically crawling out of the woodwork.'

"'It's easy,' Chuck told him. 'Ask out a hundred girls and at least five of them are going to say yes.'

"'Are you serious?' my brother yelped. He was very incredulous. 'Doesn't that mean that ninety-five say no?'

"'Give or take,' Chuck answered nonchalantly.

"'Ouch!' my brother commented.

"'Well, just think about it,' Chuck went on. 'You've got four weekends, four Saturday nights a month . . .'

"'And *five* dates,' my brother chimed in, beginning to see Chuck's logic.

"'More than enough,' Chuck replied. Then he took aim and sank one from what would have been half-court, nothing but net.

"I never forgot that conversation," says Cindy. "I didn't begin dating seriously until I was in college, but after spending one too many Saturday nights doing my laundry, I thought why not trot out Chuck's theory, give it a go, and see where it lands me.

"I didn't actually ask out a hundred guys, or anything near that when I first started out," Cindy explains. "I also wanted to figure out how to make my method appear a little less formal. Instead of finding ways to ask guys out, I decided to put myself in the path of lots of likely candidates and just let the scenario develop naturally.

"Eventually, I picked out my first test case, a boy in my philosophy class, and asked him if he wanted to study with me for a test we had coming up. He said sure. After a few hours in the library stacks, we went out for coffee at the campus center. It was a pleasant time, and I left it at that.

"I ran into the next guy on line at the cafeteria. Or to be more specific, he ran into me," she recalls with a smile. "He wasn't looking where he was going and spilled his lunch tray all over my sneakers. He was horrified, but I couldn't help laughing. He was so sweet and apologetic that I asked him to join me for lunch. We became really good buddies, nothing romantic though.

"The third guy I met in the gym. I was doing some weight training and asked him if he'd mind spotting me for the bench press. We got to talking, and hit it off really well. There was a dance coming up that weekend at the campus union, and I let him know I would be there, which, since I was already planning to attend with my roommate, was the truth. I wasn't exactly asking him out, I was giving him the option. No pressure.

"Well, he showed up! That night became our first official date. We went out for the rest of the school year until we graduated. It wasn't a lifelong romance for either of us, and we knew it, but we really enjoyed it while it lasted.

"So now whenever I'm between beaus," Cindy concludes, "I thank Chuck—who is now happily married and the father of four, by the way—and follow the advice he gave my brother all those years ago. I haven't found my one true love yet, but I've met tons of great guys, and I figure, the more I'm out there, the better chance I have of being in the right place at the right time when the real thing comes along."

2. Accept rejection.

While some maintain that men don't feel the pain of rejection and suffer the throes of torment when love goes wrong, in fact there's evidence that suggests that men take breaking up, divorce, death, or other traumatic forms of separation much harder than women, and they don't bounce back nearly as well, either.

However, in the dating zone, men don't sweat the little stuff or take things as personally as women do. It's not that they're insensitive; it's more of a water-off-a-duck's-back thing, a built-in defense mechanism that keeps them from getting hurt too often. This Teflon phenomenon can be a useful tool to keep us from getting stuck in a wad of gooey self-pity and doubt when things don't go the way we'd like them to in the game of love.

Lots of women have an unhealthy habit of investing time and emotion in men they barely know on the chance that something may come of it. They build these situations up in their minds until the fantasy supplants the reality. Then, if it doesn't work out, their hopes are dashed and their feelings devastated. It's much better to try to take a leaf from the pages of the book men read from. Stay in the moment and focus on the here and now, instead of the what might be, and you'll greatly reduce the chances of running into disaster.

If you ask a man out and he's not interested, move on. There's no point in spending endless hours trying to figure out where you went wrong, or what you could have done to make him want you. Chances are, it wasn't anything personal. You just didn't light his lights. It happens.

If a man doesn't want you, it's not the end of the world. Like the old song says, you've got to "pick yourself up, dust yourself off, and start all over again."

3. Be direct.

This is fairly self-explanatory, but many women from the time they hit puberty until the day they check into the nursing home would rather shave their underarms with a dull butter knife than let a man know up front that they're interested in him. You know the drill: You ask your best friend Joe to ask his lab partner Marty if he's ever talked about you and what, if anything, Marty's said. If Marty's interested, then his envoy comes and asks the girl who sits next to you in homeroom whether or not she knows if you already have a date for the spring formal. Word goes back to him that you've had a few nibbles but no direct bites, and then, if all goes well, he finally asks you out for the big night.

This is all well and good in high school or even college, since everybody knows everybody, or at least knows someone who knows someone who knows everybody, but once you get outside that small insular environment, you'll probably find that you're on your own. If you haven't learned the value of being direct, you'll spend a lot of valuable time treading water when you could be diving deep into a pool of meaningful love — or at least, hot sex.

One of the biggest differences between the way men and women are raised is that boys are put on the fast track to be challenge-oriented and success-driven. From the earliest moments of their education, boys spend their formative years honing competitive skills that will help them get ahead in sports, academics, and social interaction. Boys are taught they should play to win.

It should be pointed out that while girls have come a long way in these areas as well, much of the time they're still playing catch-up. This is because it's really only recently that we women have given ourselves permission to want as much or to work as hard as our male counterparts, especially when it comes to dating. We're still afraid we won't be considered feminine if we are too outspoken in our desires. The trick is to discern the difference between being aggressive and being assertive: in being aggressive we ignore the needs of others in favor of our own; in being assertive, we merely state our needs clearly in the hope that others will comply. Comprendo?

The bottom line is, it doesn't hurt to ask. Not that you should go throwing yourself into some fellow's lap or hiring a billboard with the message "Harry, want to go out with me? Dial 1-800-I'M-YOURS . . . Regards, Phyllis" painted on it in twenty-foot letters. You can be direct and subtle at the same time. Most guys don't have to be hit over the head to catch a clue that you're interested. Just find a nice way to let him know and take it from there.

If you've never tried approaching a man before, or are still having a hard time making the distinction between assertive and aggressive behavior, think for a minute about all the different pickup techniques—from the sublime to the ridiculous—that men have used on you. Consider what got you hot and what left you cold. For instance, construction sites are rife with cat-callers and come-on lines. It's almost impossible for a woman to walk by one and not get propositioned by at least one of the workers. These experiences can range from humiliating and infuriating to downright touching and sincere, depending on the guy, of course.

"I'll never forget that summer day I was walking through Manhattan, on my way to interview a city bureaucrat about landlord housing violations for a piece I was writing," recounts a freelance journalist, Inez. "There was a huge hole, almost a block long, where a row of buildings had been demolished and new construction was going up. The sidewalk was all chopped up, which made for pretty rough going in my high-heeled pumps. As I was passing a gate in the fence, I noticed a few crew workers loitering around, and I knew I was in for it.

"One fat slug with a three-day growth and a beer gut the size of a grand piano pointed to his crotch and yelled, 'Hey, honey, bet you'd *love* to get a piece of *this* meat!' It got so rude I can't repeat the rest of what they said. I was so upset I was practically in tears. Then, wouldn't you know it, my heel broke. They just laughed and jeered and kept up with their nasty suggestions. At that point, I did start to cry.

"That's when one of them broke away from the crowd and walked over with this big smile on his face. I have to tell you, I was expecting the worst, but this guy just said, 'May I?,' took the shoe, knocked the heel back in with a hammer that was hanging on his tool belt, and handed it back to me. I was stunned. Then he pulled a bandanna out of his back pocket and offered it to me. 'Go ahead, blow,' he said. 'It's wrinkled, but it's clean.'

"I had to laugh. That's exactly what my mom always said when she unearthed a scrunched-up Kleenex from her purse to wipe our noses with. 'That's better,' he told me. 'You know, you've really got a lovely smile.' I'm sure that while this exchange was going on, his buddies were still yelling and carrying on, but I didn't hear them. That simple act of kindness opened a door to my heart. I started to thank him and hand him back the bandanna, but he told me to keep it 'and the next time you need a knight in shining armor,' he joked, 'just stand across the street and raise the banner. I'll be there.' Then he just turned around and walked back behind the fence and out of sight.

"After the interview—which went really well despite my teary mascara—I felt happy and kind of keyed up. I was free for the next few hours, but I decided to look at my appointment calendar to double-check where my next meeting was. Instead of a little black book, I pulled out that construction worker's bandanna, and found myself smiling all over again.

"I wasn't sure if his offer had been a serious one, but I decided to take him up on it. On my way back to the construction site, I stopped in a hardware store and bought a mop handle, tied the bandanna to one end of it, then parked myself across the street from the gate and started to wave the thing around. After a few minutes, I began to feel really silly and I was about to leave, when all of a sudden, there he was, dodging traffic, headed straight for me. By the time he got to me, he was pretty much out of breath, but smiling.

"'Do knights in shining armor take time off to eat lunch?' I asked him. It seems they did. And that's how I met Sam . . . my husband."

Now, technically, Sam was the one who made the first move here, but there's still a lot we can learn by his example. Simple acts of kindness, when they come from the heart, not from a calculating mind, make a great first impression. And while waving a banner the way Inez did may be extreme, just saying something as fundamental as "I think you're a very attractive man. Would you care to have a cup of coffee with me?" can work, too.

Another woman who champions the direct approach is Irene. "I was taking a night class in art history," she recalls, "and found myself seated next to an unbelievably amazing man. Truly, he had one of the most brilliant minds I've ever encountered. The witty comments he made were so razor-sharp, they often left me weak with laughter. Trouble was, I couldn't tell what team he was playing on—meaning, I didn't know whether he preferred boys or girls. Eventually, I decided to just ask him.

"One night after class, I walked up to him and said point-blank, 'If you're straight, I'd like to date you. If you're gay, I'd love to be your friend.' Thinking back on it now, had he been straight, perhaps he would have found my declaration offensive, but it turned out he preferred the company of boys, at least romantically speaking. He did, however, become—and has remained—one of my dearest friends.

"I'm very comfortable giving voice to my feelings when I meet a man in whom I'm interested. It's my view that as long as a woman is polite, presents herself with sincerity, and steers clear of vulgarity, she should state her case and see what happens."

If you find these methods too daunting, don't worry. There are other simple, direct techniques—some low-key and some less so—that will help you to meet members of the opposite sex in a manner that suits your personal style, whatever it may be.

Getting His Attention

When it comes to flirting, the basics are really the best place to start. Simple things you do in your day-to-day life can be applied to piquing a man's interest, or you can try something more daring if you're up to it.

Smile.

If you're at all interested in a man, smile. Not the vacant "An alien life form has swooped down in a saucer and lobotomized me" smile; not the pained "Help, I'm being held captive at my seven-year-old cousin's piano recital" smile; not the even more pained "I'm rolling my eyes in my head and you couldn't possibly be more boring so why doesn't the earth open up and swallow you?" smile. It has to be a real one—teeth are optional. You don't have to keep grinning like an idiot. As long as he sees you, a brief upward curl of the lip will do. You get ten extra points for tossing in an expression that says, *I know something you don't know, but you'd love to find out.*

Even if the man you happen to be smiling at doesn't turn out to be the man of your dreams, a smile tells him that you're at least approachable and that you won't shoot him out of the water before he gets his pickup line out of its holster.

Make eye contact.

The time to gaze longingly at a man is over a romantic dinner, not before you've met. In flirting, eye contact should initially be like tag. One quick hit, then he's it. A fast take, then you're it. If you're doing this right and tossing in that smile we talked about, eventually this will escalate into something that more closely resembles a tennis match. Your volleys will become more intense, more direct, until finally one or the other of you will come up to the net to shake hands, or chat, or exchange numbers—whatever it takes to see where you can go from there.

Buy him a drink.

Again, turning the tables can sometimes work like a charm. Men like attention. They are easily flattered. Unless he's a Neanderthal, this gesture will not send him screaming out into the night. It will show him that you're generous and impetuous—not a bad combination.

Now, as every woman who has ever been in a bar knows, accepting a drink is not necessarily an open invitation to romance. A man, like a woman, may appreciate the gesture, but may not be looking for anything more. If that turns out to be the case, it's time to break out your Teflon gear and exit gracefully.

Smoke a cigar!

Sorry, Grandma Clara! I hate to break it to you, but a woman smoking a cigar, especially in a provocative manner, can be a major turn-on to men. And as evidenced by the huge proliferation of chic cigar bars across the country, this is one hot fad that may be here to stay. Does cigar smoking have phallic implications? You'd better believe it, so this one may not be for the faint of heart. Don't, can't, or won't smoke? An ice-cream cone, though not as trendy, can garner similar results. And, of course, there's always that old standby, the banana — although it is fairly hard to savor a piece of fruit in quite the same way as a fine cigar.

Start a conversation.

Think first, then just speak. ("Hi," followed by babbling, is not what we're after.) Compliment him on something he's wearing. Look over his shoulder at the newspaper he's reading and comment about one of the headlines. Ask for directions. Let the situation you're in inspire you: whether you're in a subway car, walking the produce aisle, or watching a baseball game, use the moment and improvise.

Seize the moment.

You never know when fate is going to toss a wonderful man in your path. So as long as your gut isn't sending you danger signals, when an opportunity comes along, sometimes you've just got to grab it. For instance:

"I was headed back to my office after an important client meeting," recalls Kaye. "I had just gotten into the lobby when, whoosh, the elevator doors opened and one of the most magnificent men I'd ever seen stepped out. He was tall, dark, handsome . . . and then some. I think my jaw actually dropped open. There was no point in pretending I wasn't staring at him—I was.

"He walked up and introduced himself to me and suddenly, I forgot all about going back up to my office. We only chatted for the briefest of moments, but I could tell there was something truly special about him. Then he told me that the limo waiting at the curb was there to take him to the airport. He was actually moving across the country! *Just my luck*, I thought. *I finally find the perfect man and he's leaving town.* But he practically pleaded with me to give him my business card. I couldn't see any harm in it, so I did. As I watched him walk out to the limo and disappear into the traffic, I felt exhilarated and frustrated at the same time.

"When I got back upstairs, my phone was ringing. It was him! He was calling me from the car phone. He was so sweet and so charming, I could have just listened to him talk for the rest of the afternoon. That two-minute chance meeting led to a year-long, long-distance romance that was so hot I'm surprised it didn't burn up the telephone wires. Eventually, we called it quits because we knew neither one of us was going to give up our career, but while it lasted, it was totally outrageous, romantic, and wonderful."

Keeping His Attention

If you take the social graces we all use in everyday life and apply them to flirting and seduction, you'll be pleasantly surprised at the great results you can achieve. A combination of good manners and common sense will go a long way toward helping you to both establish and maintain romantic interest.

Be inclusive.

To create an atmosphere of camaraderie with a new man, do your best to make him feel that he's in on the joke, not that the joke is on him. Ask for his opinion. See what things you have in common and explore them, but try to avoid being judgmental about your differences.

Pay attention.

One thing most men love is a good listener. You should be as interested in hearing about him as he is in finding out about you. When a man is talking, let him talk. Don't keep interrupting or feeling the need to one-up him. You'll have plenty of opportunity to talk about yourself. Remember, good conversations, like good relationships, rely on give and take. If the seesaw only leans to one side, neither party will be interested for very long.

Find the humor.

There is no need to be dead serious 100 percent of the time. Hell, maybe not even 50 percent. When dating is new and things are spontaneous, unexpected things, for good or ill, are bound to occur. You can either face them as if you're trapped in the last act of a Greek tragedy, or you can find the humor and continue to enjoy each other's company. We live in a very blame-oriented society, and when something goes amiss, it's almost always our first instinct to start pointing fingers. Next time, when something goes awry, instead of fretting and fuming and puffing yourself up like a prize pigeon, why not try humor instead? Nothing can defuse a tense situation more quickly than a good laugh.

Expand Your Dating Horizons

How often have you caught yourself beginning a sentence with the words "I'd never go out with a man who . . ." How often have you turned down a date with someone who didn't fit into your prefabricated, fixed set of notions of what was "suitable" for you? If you're one of those people who've always thought that dating had to lead to something bigger, try to let that go for a while. Not every liaison has to have grand implications, and not every man you go out with must be the potential Mr. to your would-be Mrs.

Back when Mary Jane was a college senior, a very handsome freshman—and I mean *very* handsome—asked her out. And she said no. Why? Because he was "too young." Having taken some semesters off to deal with family problems, M.J.—as her friends called her—was about eighteen months older than the average upperclassman. This gap, M.J. reasoned ("wrongly so," she admits ruefully), made her more worldly and mature than the rest of the student body. To date someone whom she classified—again, mistakenly—as a mere "boy" was out of the question.

Meanwhile, M.J.'s would-be suitor was charming, bright, funny—oh, did I mention really handsome?—and very determined to change her mind. He courted her with flowers (no small feat on an undergrad's budget). He wrote her funny little notes. He carried her laundry. In short, he was a real gem. But M.J. had convinced herself that he wasn't right for her because of the vast difference in their ages—"which, come to think of it, must have been all of three and a half years," she now concedes with a laugh.

"Eventually," M.J. relates, "he took the hint and went off in search of someone who would appreciate him, not for his date of birth, but for what made him such a great guy. And he found her. I used to see them walking around campus, holding hands and gazing at one another so blissfully it was enough to make you sick. But the thing that really caught in my throat—apart from having to lug around my own laundry—was the fact that it could have been me. Instead of being part of a happy couple, I was alone with my principles. And some principles can make for pretty cold bedfellows."

Especially when those principles are based in a belief system that is flawed or biased to begin with. "Had I cheated myself out of a great love affair? Who's to say?" M.J. muses. "But one day I woke up and the truth struck me like a wet mackerel. I'd let a great guy walk out of my life because I'd allowed myself to think that only men who matched up with some weird little checklist I'd concocted for myself were worthy of me. I began to wonder where I'd come up with this stuff. And it dawned on me that I'd been cutting off my nose to spite my face."

While it's true that hanging out with ne'er-do-wells and abusers is not a good investment of anyone's time or affections, M.J.'s problem wasn't having limits as to what was and wasn't acceptable in a man, but how narrowly she'd defined those limits. By predetermining that only men who met her strict criteria were datable, she'd closed the book on more than a few really good ones without even so much as cracking the cover to see if what they had inside might be intriguing, exciting, or, ultimately, satisfying. Who knows what wonderful things she missed—and you might be missing—by not letting yourself be open to life's endless possibilities?

These days, M.J. and her husband Stan have been happily married for six years. Who's the elder of the pair? "Let's just say I *learned* from my mistakes," M.J. concedes.

Another woman who nearly talked herself out of a great relationship before it started was Lauren. From the time she was a little girl, Lauren's parents had taught her to have very high expectations of herself and of those around her. She deserved only the best things life had to offer; to accept anything less was to settle. As she grew up, Lauren became an overachiever. Any grade less than an A was not good enough for her. She was editor of her yearbook, president of the science club, and valedictorian at her class graduation.

Lauren did some dating in high school and was fairly popular, but she knew that she wasn't ready for anything serious. Getting into a good university was what she focused most of her energies on, and with her immaculate grade-point average and near-perfect S.A.T. scores, the Ivy League welcomed her with open arms.

In college, Lauren continued to excel. Her love of science quickly led her to choose premed for her major. Again, she graduated at the head of her class, was accepted at the finest medical school, and, though she had to work like a dog, completed her internship and residency with flying colors. Needless to say, when Lauren and her family learned that she had been selected from a field of several hundred top competitors to join the surgical staff of a world-renowned teaching hospital, they were all elated.

For the next year, she threw herself totally into the hospital routine. But eventually, her all-work-and-no-play lifestyle began to leave her feeling that she was missing out on something. Lauren, who had held herself aloof for such a long time, realized that she now craved intimacy. She wanted a man in her life, but according to the tenets her parents had taught her, she could only date "the best"—the best being her equal or better, job-, salary-, and status-wise.

Lauren was an attractive woman. She'd never had a lack of offers or opportunities when it came to men, and now she was finally ready to accept some. Friends introduced her to eligible candidates. Whenever she attended a medical convention or a hospital function, she kept her eyes peeled for potential romantic partners. She spent more than a few evenings at her college alumni club, checking out the members. Her networking efforts were rewarded with some pleasant dates, newfound professional contacts, and even a few good investment tips, but no passion. Though the men she was meeting could hold their own on an intellectual level, none of the "best" men clicked for her in the chemistry department.

One Friday night, after the end of a particularly dismal date with an egomaniacal astrophysicist, Lauren decided that since she was off-duty the next day, rather than go home, she'd treat herself to an espresso and pastry at the café that had opened up in her neighborhood several months previously. In truth, Lauren had become something of a weekend regular at the place, reading the Sunday paper and sipping herbal tea for a couple of hours to unwind. Never having been there at night before, she was a little surprised to find a poetry reading in progress when she walked in, but she figured the poems would give her something to think about besides her evening's dating fiasco, so she sat down and placed an order.

Just as the waitress put the demitasse of steaming, ink-black liquid and a thick slice of cheesecake down in front of Lauren, the poet who had been reading finished her selection to polite applause and exited the makeshift stage. The spotlight dimmed and there seemed to be no further action, so Lauren lost herself in the restaurant's cheerful hubbub and allowed herself to fall into the sensual comfort of the luscious dessert.

When the lights came back up, the most stunning man Lauren had ever beheld was standing on the stage. The spotlight illuminated his mane of dark, curly hair, making him look for all the world like a naughty angel with a silvery halo. *You've been watching too much TV*, Lauren told herself . . . and then she recognized him. It was Billy, one of the waiters who worked there—the one she often overtipped because he was cute.

As Billy began to read from his work, Lauren found herself unable to take her eyes off him. The poetry was at one moment playful and witty, the next moment steaming with sensual longing. It was unlike anything she'd ever heard before—not that she'd ever spent too much time on poetry—and she was enchanted. In the middle of one particularly erotic passage, Billy looked up and caught her eye. For the rest of the reading, it seemed as if he were directing his attention only to her.

When he was finished, he walked over to her table and spoke. "What's up, doc? Mind if I have a seat?" She gestured for him to sit down. The attraction between them was so thick you could have used it to put up wallpaper. Lauren managed to tell Billy how wonderful she thought his poetry was.

"Thanks," he said, taking her hand. "It's just a pity that art doesn't always pay the rent."

"But you're so talented," she pressed. "Surely you can get your work published."

"I have," he replied with a wry smile, "but there's almost nobody who makes a living as a poet these days. . . . I'll tell you a secret," he said, leaning in so close that Lauren felt faint with pleasure. "I was a stockbroker for a few years after I got out of school, and I was the golden boy. I was on the fast track to a junior partnership in one of the hot new houses . . . but I hated it. I don't know which suits gave me more grief—the ones I had to wear or the ones I was working for. Everything was dog-eat-dog and politics. You were only as valuable as your last big win. You could've been Jack the Ripper as long as you were making money, and it wouldn't have made any difference to the bosses. So, one day I just walked out . . . and I've never looked back, except with relief."

Lauren's mind was suddenly filled with confusion. Finally, here was a man she wanted—*really wanted*—and he was content being a "waiter-slash-poet." How could she justify that? How could she ever feel comfortable knowing that her salary so far outdistanced his? How could she reconcile knowing that her social obligations would take her places where dating a man like this might be sneered at? Fortunately for Lauren, she was saved by the bell, or in her case, the beeper. "It's the hospital," Lauren told Billy. "I'm being paged to an emergency. I've got to go."

"How about letting me fix you dinner next week?" Billy asked. "I'm a great cook."

By that point, Lauren didn't know what she wanted. "I . . . um, well . . . my schedule is . . ." she stammered.

Registering her indecision, Billy quickly reversed gears. "That's okay," he told her. "Maybe I'll see you Sunday for some Red Zinger and the *Times* crossword."

"Yeah, maybe," she said. She could tell he was disappointed, perhaps even a little bit hurt. So, after saying good-bye with as much haste as she could manage without appearing impolite, she lit out of there as fast as her legs would carry her.

It was nearly 3 A.M. when she finally made it back to her apartment, but even though she was exhausted, she couldn't sleep. An odd litany of words kept running through her head — a refrain from the devil's own lullaby: *Good, better, best. Never let them rest, 'til the good is the better and the better is the best.* She recognized who the singers were. They were her mom and dad. *But what is the best?* Lauren pondered, finally dropping off to sleep as the dawn nudged its way under her window shade.

On Sunday, Lauren picked up her paper as usual and began to head off toward the café, fully intending to apologize to Billy and make up some sort of acceptable excuse as to why she couldn't go out with him. But as she began to spin an appropriate tale in her head, she suddenly stopped. *Why am I doing this?* she thought. *He's a wonderful guy. After all, I'm certainly not planning to marry my mom and dad. . . .*

Filled with unexpected resolve, she found herself practically marching to the coffee shop. When she got to the threshold, her old values reared their ugly heads and whispered, *But he's a loser. . . .*

Lauren paused, frozen, not going forward, not going back. But all at once, she caught sight of Billy and the little nagging doubts in her head melted faster than a wicked witch on a waterslide.

Billy motioned her toward a table. "What's up, doc? Having the usual?"

"No," she replied firmly, "something completely different. What time do you get off?"

"Excuse me?" Billy replied, not believing his ears. Lauren repeated the question. "Seven," he told her.

"Dinner?" she asked, but it wasn't really a question.

"You mean that meal after lunch?" he teased.

"Yeah. With me. Pick you up at seven?"

"It's a date," said Billy. And it was. The first of many.

So, the next time you meet a man who interests you, but you find yourself thinking, *He's really great, but I can't go out with him because he's . . .* unless you're filling in the blank with "an ax murderer," why not give the guy a chance instead of the boot? If you're thirty-five, go ahead and grab a pizza with that cute guy who's ten years your junior. If you're a high-powered attorney, there's no law against dating a bartender. Don't say "no" before you've given "yes" a shot. Go ahead and date unusual men. You might find something wonderful—even love—in a place you'd never dreamed of looking before.

CHAPTER EIGHT

Playing Against the Rules

AHEM. DO ANY OF THESE marching orders sound familiar?

- Ask him out? No way!
- Ask him to dance? Forget it!
- Memorize these words: "I'm sorry, my phone only takes incoming calls . . ."
- Never pay for anything or offer to split the check.
- Don't sleep with him on the first, second, or even the third date.
- Never be the first to say I love you, and whatever you do, don't be the one to bring up moving in, marriage, or kids.

If you're seriously committed to making romance a part of your life, then by now it's a good bet that you've already read the rules, cracked the code, toed the line, followed the leader, inserted flap A into slot B, studied the handbook, and maybe even taken a couple of refresher courses. However, until we learn to define romance for ourselves—to figure out what we expect to put into it and what we hope to get out of it—what we may be constructing for ourselves is not a home for love, but a house of cards. It may look sturdy enough on the surface, but can it stand the tests of time, truth, and for-better-or-worse?

Now may be a good time to ask yourself, "Whose love is it, anyway?" Just whose ideal are you striving to create (or, in so many cases, recreate)? Your parents'? Your peers'? Your lover's? We all have a picture in our minds of the perfect relationship. We've all got boundaries, and it's only common sense to make them known early on. But when you look at the list above—don't ask him out, don't call him, don't pay for anything—are those really your don'ts, or are they coming to you direct from the Grandma Zone? Sure, a lot of women swear by their rules, but a lot more— plus most men—just want to swear *at* them. You really don't have to play along with these cat-and-mouse games to be successful in love—unless you're hankering to step into a time machine, that is.

Yes, the throwback guys are still out there—the Ward Cleavers, the Ozzie Nelsons, the Ralph Kramdens of the world—and really, they're not all such a bad lot. But if you're in the market for a man who is looking for more than just "the little woman," it's time to say "Good night, Gracie," and find yourself a lover who happily seeks a mate who is more than a mere extension of his own ego. (The good news is, they're out there, too!)

To that end, what follows is a list of "anti-rules"— common-sense advice on how to hook up with a man without having to "hook him." It's time to stop worrying about playing hard to get, being easy to be with, and pretending to be something you're not. Be who you are, say what you think, and the rest will fall into place.

"How's seven-thirty?"

Here's a scenario: You've gone to the supermarket to do your Saturday morning grocery shopping. You're in the beverage aisle, and the juvenile delinquent who passes for a store manager has fiendishly put all the diet cola on the top shelf, beyond the reach of anyone who isn't a professional basketball player. There isn't a stock clerk in sight.

Suddenly, while you're considering your dilemma, wondering how you can possibly balance yourself between your shopping cart and the bottom shelf long enough to snag the bottle you're after without dragging the entire contents of the display down on your head, a point guard from the Chicago Bulls (or fill in the team of your choice) steps up behind you, and in his deep, masculine voice, says, "Can I get that for you?"

He passes you the bottle and you thank him. The dreamboat then says, "I hope you don't mind, but I wonder if you might help me. I'm picking up some groceries for my folks and my mom asked me to get her a spaghetti squash—dad's on a low-carb diet—only I haven't the faintest idea what that is, much less how to pick out a good one."

Since you were headed to the produce department anyway, you offer to accompany him and aid him in his vegetable quest. After giving it the thump, sniff, and thumbprint test, you hand him the nicest specimen you can find. It's at this point that you realize that not only is he grateful, he's interested in more than just squash. You stand there and talk for a while, and one topic leads to another. "Listen," he finally says, "I know it's short notice, but would you like to have dinner with me tonight? It doesn't have to be anything fancy. I'd just like to get to know you better."

Your heart is singing, *Yes, yes, yes!* But in your mind, Grandma's voice is screaming, *No, no, no!* Don't listen to her. You *can* accept a date on the spur of the moment and still get respect from a man. (Just remember to use the dating commandments. Apply common sense and keep yourself safe. If you've just met a man, no matter how nice he may seem, he's still a stranger. Don't hop into his car, go to his place, or let him pick you up where you live until you know a little more about him.) Maura's romance with Michael is a good case in point.

"It was Christmas season, nearly twenty years ago," recounts Maura. "I'd just graduated from college, was working a part-time job, and still lived at home with my parents. Since I had a lot more leisure than money in those days, most of the presents I gave people were made by hand. One afternoon, I'd gone into the neighborhood notions store to pick up some ribbon and lace to finish off the vest I was sewing for my brother's fiancée.

"I must've been there for nearly an hour. Even now, there's something about those places I find hypnotic. One look at all the patterns and the textures and colors, and my mind takes over with a million projects I want to start . . . most of which I never get to. But that day, as I was standing in a little alcove, looking up at a rainbow wall of different-colored buttons, I realized that there was a man standing next to me and he was smiling.

"He was kind of tall—maybe six feet. His hair was dirty blond and he had on a green army-surplus jacket. He looked more than a little like Donald Sutherland in *M*A*S*H* (that's the movie version, for all you twentysome-things who grew up thinking the only man who ever played Hawkeye was Alan Alda), and when he spoke, his voice had a similar, sexy timbre—minus the Canadian accent. 'Guess how much I paid for this jacket?' he asked.

"Due to my limited budget," Maura explains, "I was a veteran of thrift shop pricing. 'Seven bucks,' I told him.

" 'How did you know that?' he asked me. I'd gotten it right to the penny. I told him I was psychic. He told me that he was Michael and he was glad to meet me. Then he said, 'You know, the only thing wrong with this coat . . .' I finished the sentence for him, 'is that it's missing some buttons.'

" 'Psychic, huh?' he joked.

" 'No, just observant,' I answered. Then he asked me if I might lend him some of my expertise in picking out the best match for the missing buttons. It was a piece of cake, really, and we both knew that he could just as easily have chosen for himself, but we were flirting in high gear and pretended not to notice. After he'd gotten the buttons down from the wall, he asked me if I'd like to go to the deli next door for a cup of coffee with him.

"I hadn't had a lot of experience with men up until then," Maura conceded, "but I remember that most of my girlfriends had made it a point that you couldn't appear eager when a guy asked you out. You were supposed to play hard to get. I guess all these things were running through my mind, and I hesitated. Michael told me he understood if I didn't want to, but he explained that he wasn't going to be in town for very long.

"I don't know what made me do it, but I said, 'Sure, let's go.' Then calamity struck. We got up to the cash register and Michael realized that he didn't have any money—he'd spent it all Christmas shopping. His family's house was only a few minutes away, and he said that if I didn't mind waiting, he could run home and get more cash. But I told him it was okay, I'd spring for the buttons *and* the coffee."

According to Maura, it turned out that the lady who ran the shop was a real angel. She let Michael pay for his two-dollar purchase with a ten-dollar check, and she gave him the change, so he wound up buying the coffee after all. They sat and talked in that deli for hours. Finally, the owner wanted to go home, and he tossed them out so he could lock up.

"Michael and I spent a lot of time together for the next few weeks," Maura recalls. "Then he had to go out of town. He was shuttling back and forth between coasts. He'd been living in California, but his dad and brother were in New York. Part of the reason he was home was to get the family business in order . . . his dad was dying of cancer. Meeting him like that was a total fluke. He was one of the finest, most decent men I've ever known—my first real boyfriend. We weren't meant to be together forever, but I always look back on that time with only the warmest of memories. . . . And to think, if I'd stuck with convention instead of following my gut, I'd never have gotten to know him at all. That would have been a huge loss. Huge."

On top of the fact that you might be missing out on something wonderful by not just saying yes now and then, there's another big really big flaw in the "You can't accept a Saturday night date after Wednesday" agenda. The whole modus operandi is rooted in the concept that we all lead nine-to-five, Monday-through-Friday lives. News flash: Not everyone has weekends free. Some great guys work the night shift. Most people in retail don't know the meaning of having Saturday and Sunday off. Lots of folks have jobs for which the schedule changes on a week-to-week, or even a day-to-day basis. And then there's overtime . . .

What do you do when suddenly your eight-hour day becomes an unexpected twelve-hour marathon? It's really hard to plan for this kind of lifestyle. But whether it's you who has nontraditional hours or your would-be lover, there's no need to shrink the number of fish in your dating pool with short-sighted thinking. Times have changed and we have to change with them.

If a man calls you up or asks you out last-minute, you've got to consider both the circumstances and his intentions. If he really wants to spend time with you and you want to spend time with him, then go for it. Being spontaneous doesn't mean you should make yourself available at a man's beck and call, but it does not make you "easy," either. There's no reason to deny both of you a shot at romance simply to prove some point that has exceeded its expiration date by a couple of decades.

Just don't forget to keep your radar up. If your love object's behavior seems to be forming a pattern you don't like, call him on it, or make other plans for the night he usually asks you out. If he's reasonable, he'll catch a clue. However, should you get the feeling he's only using you as his fall-back date and truly *is* taking you for granted, then you're perfectly justified in sending him on his way.

"May I have this dance?"

You're at a club with a gaggle of girlfriends. The pulse of the music is deep in your bones and your hips sway back and forth to its rhythm. As you chat with your pals, you can't help but notice that cute guy across the room. When next you look up, he seems to be smiling at you; then he turns his head back to the conversation he's having with his buddies. A minute later the same thing happens. You return the smile, then listen politely as your friend Louise fills you in on the details of her latest fling. You look up again just as he does. Your eyes lock, you both blush a little. The music is more urgent now, pulling your body with an unseen cord to fall into the beat. You want to dance . . . with him. Your mind is racing. *Should I? Should I? Should I?* it says. You point to him, then crook your index finger three times quick. "Who me?" he mouths silently from across the room. You nod in assent. And then you both begin to walk, slowly and with purpose, to the center of the dance floor. His extended hand meets yours in one fluid motion. You fall into each other's arms and . . .

What's wrong with this picture? Well, according to a lot of guys, absolutely nothing. But isn't there a basic taboo about a woman asking a man to dance?

"Only if she insists on leading," quips Jim, a yet-to-be-married film editor. "I think it's great when it happens,

even when I'm not interested in anything more, but especially when I am. Some men — like me — don't always
want to have to make the first move. And let me tell you,
not all of us suffer from that *If I can have it, I don't want it*
complex. I'm not going to throw out a chance for something special just because it came to me, rather than me
having to go to it."

But don't guys assume that a woman who asks a man
is probably a tad . . . desperate?

"No one is going to think that just because a woman
asks you to dance, five minutes later she's going to want
to marry you," Jim says. "To me, the really hopeless case
is the one who sits in the corner waiting all night for
someone to ask *her* to dance . . . or someone who does ask
you, but with an attitude like you've already said no. A
chip on the shoulder is definitely *not* an attractive acces-
sory. But when a woman asks me to dance like she *means*
it . . .well, I love that. It tells me a lot about her. She's confident. She knows what she wants and she isn't afraid to
go after it. I'll let you in on a secret," he confesses in a
mock whisper. "More often than not, that translates into
the bedroom as well. C'mon, a woman who actually lets
you know what she wants instead of me having to
fumpher around guessing? That's pure gold."

It's Your Call

Consider the following three hypothetical situations:

#1. You go to pick up your car from your mechanic.
Though you've never told him so, you've secretly had a
crush on him for a couple of months now. His favorite
band is coming to town for a concert to which you have
an extra ticket. You "happen to find out" that he isn't seeing anyone. Do you call him?

#2. You're at a bar after work just hanging out with your crew. An incredibly handsome swain sends a cocktail your way, then comes over to introduce himself. You chat amiably for a while while your hormones swing into overdrive. After a few minutes, he says, "This is awful. I wasn't expecting to meet anyone as wonderful as you tonight. I really have to be across town at a fund-raising banquet in fifteen minutes. Here's my card. Call me." Do you call him?

#3. You finally met Mr. Right—okay, Mr. Maybe. Last night, you spent a near-perfect evening together, and that near-perfect included some great sex. You're an adult. You know the difference between a mere mind-blowing session of getting your jollies and the real thing—and this felt so real you think you might be dreaming. Do you call him?

Answers:

#1: Yes, you call him! Why else did you bother to "find out" if he had a girlfriend? This kind of date is also a lot less threatening to a man than, say, going out to dinner and a movie. At best, you'll have a really great time; at worst, you'll be two people hanging out enjoying the music. It's very low pressure. It can work.

A possible drawback? Some people say that boyfriends are a dime a dozen, but a good mechanic is one in a million. Have him rebuild your transmission *before* you go out with him—just in case.

#2: Yes, you call him! There's at least a fifty-fifty chance that he wasn't really expecting to meet someone as wonderful as you that night, and he really did have to dash off. If he was just handing you a line? It happens. If he wasn't, why not try to see him again? Who knows, he might be the most wonderful person *you've* met in a long time, too.

#3: Yes, you call him—but this is the tricky one. A lot of people are going to scream, "No! No! No! You've got to wait until *he* calls *you*." Not really. The problems most women run into when they reach out and touch someone aren't about the "her calling him" thing, but rather, what she says when she does.

It's fine to pick up the phone and call a man to say hello or to tell him you had a really great time; just don't make it sound as if you've already started planning your future together. Don't fish around for hints about his feelings for you, and whatever you do, if you get his answering machine, don't call him every fifteen minutes until he picks up. Smothering is not a trait men look for in a woman.

Just be cool and cut him some slack, and after you've made that first call, it really is a good idea to wait until *he* gets back to *you*.

"Check, please!"

The die-hard convention that men must pay for the pleasure of our company is one that, as much as we keep beating it over the head with a shovel, refuses to go gentle into that good night. There are women who still insist that in order for men to show that they value us, they must fork over the cash—or the plastic—to prove it. But these women who are looking to be "prized" may in reality be relegating themselves to the status of a trophy. And a loving cup by any other name is still only an empty, ornamental vessel, commemorating the vanity of the man who has won it. I'd call that a booby prize.

Thankfully, along with the nine-to-five world, going the way of the dodo is the notion that men control the money. Yes, statistically speaking they do earn X amount more on average than we do, but with the number of women in the workforce at a record high and still climbing, the income differences are finally leveling out.

Ultimately, money is about power, and whoever commands it controls the playing field. When women finally attained mastery over their own finances for the first time, they found they were not only *getting a chance to*, but *having to* make the choices that go with it. While it's true that some of them tossed back this newfound responsibility like a hot potato with cries of "I don't want to fend for myself! I want somebody to take care of me," a lot of others, understanding that economic freedom leads to personal autonomy, took the ball and ran with it.

"When I pay my own way," explains Lillian, a twenty-nine-year-old pediatric nurse, "I don't ever have to feel that I 'owe' someone something. There are some guys who will take you places and *not* expect anything, who do it because that's the way they were raised and they actually think it's the right thing to do. But there are just as many jerks out there who think that if they buy you dinner, you owe them sex. Well, I can buy my own dinner, thank you. And if I want to sleep with you after dessert, that's strictly up to me."

Sandra, a thirty-six-year-old marketing vice president, has another take on taking the check. "Some of the men I've gone out with," she says, "make a big deal out of paying for *everything*. If you offer to split a check—or, God forbid!—pick it up, they go practically ballistic. It's like you're insulting their manhood. I've learned not to argue with gentlemen like that. If that's what they want, then so be it, and good for them. Who am I to turn down a lobster dinner?

"On the other hand, I don't have any problem chipping in for my share or even taking a guy out and paying for the whole evening. Last year, I was dating an actor. Brilliant talent, negligible bank account. He paid when he could, and I made sure not to rub his nose in it when he couldn't. Money was never an issue between us. The bottom line is, I make a lot and I enjoy spending it. You should judge a man by what he's got in his heart and in his head, not what he's got in his wallet. Mind you, I have zero tolerance for freeloaders, but it doesn't matter who pulls out the gold card, as long as a man is okay with me paying, I'm okay with it, too."

In this day and age, there really is no need for the man to foot the bill while the woman sits there like a lox. And you know what? Some men don't mind having the tables turned once in a while. Just listen to what Ted, a high-level entertainment attorney, had to say: "I've dated a fair number of women over the last few years, and it's funny, it didn't matter if it was for coffee, brunch, bowling, or a night on the town, not one of them ever offered to pop for so much as the tip. Maybe it shouldn't have bothered me, but it did. My dates just assumed that as the man, I was expected to 'put out'—so to speak. It just seemed hypocritical. I mean, after all, here were these women, making as much or more than I was, who wouldn't cough up change for the parking meter. Okay, so I'm exaggerating, but that's how it felt. Until I met Wendy, that is."

The difference between Wendy and the other women Ted had been seeing came, not at the end of their first date, but as it began. "Wendy and I had been fixed up by some mutual friends. We'd talked a few times and had arranged to meet. The day we were supposed to get together, anything that could go wrong, did. I got out to my car not only to find that my tail-lights had been smashed but, to add insult to injury, I'd gotten a ticket for it! I was livid. On my way to the office, I stopped off to get coffee and the girl behind the counter didn't put the lid on right. It exploded all over my good pants and some important documents that were on my desk . . . and things just kind of went downhill from there."

After the coffee fiasco, Ted called Wendy up on the verge of postponing the date, but she was so nice and so sympathetic that he calmed down and they decided to go ahead with their plans. That night, when she met him at the restaurant, she handed him a bouquet of daffodils. "Daffodils!" he exclaims. "No one had ever done something like that for me before. Maybe it was kind of offbeat, but it really touched me, and cheered me up, too." The evening was fast turning out to be a completely new experience for Ted, one he found himself enjoying a great deal.

"Well, let's see . . . drinks, dinner, wine, conversation, dessert, coffee, and . . . no check. I start scoping out the room, looking for the waiter," Ted recounts. "Then, Wendy reaches over, puts her hand on top of mine, and says, 'I've already taken care of it. You were having such a bad day, I thought you needed someone to make a little fuss over you.' I was floored. Good floored, that is. We've been going out for almost a year now. We haven't got any set formula for who pays for what, but I've never been happier. Wendy is definitely the best thing that's ever happened to me."

What it all boils down to is that the question of who pays ought to be approached on a case-by-case basis. If a man does insist on picking up the tab, let him — provided that you are both clear that he's doing so out of the goodness of his heart, and not because he expects something in return. If you've never considered paying at least part of your dating tuition, you might want to rethink your strategy. It's a nice change for men not to be expected to fork out a fortune to win your affections — a change many of them appreciate and will pay you back for in ways much more rewarding than mere money.

To bed or not to bed?

Claudia is on a first date with a new man, Terrence, and so far, it's been one of the most incredible nights of her life. Everything, from the appetizers to the dessert, has been perfect. The conversation has been ripe with innuendo, the chemistry undeniable. She adores everything about him, from his quirky sense of humor to the

funny way his hair pokes up at the back. The evening is
drawing to a close. It's practically all she can do to keep
from taking him right there on the table. Somehow, the
check gets paid, and the couple walks outside. Being a
gentleman, Terrence offers to see Claudia home. When he
takes her hand in the taxi, she melts into a puddle of bliss.
Then he kisses her, and the puddle begins to simmer. The
cab pulls up in front of Claudia's building. It's clear that
neither one of them wants the date to end.

Does she invite him up to make wild, passionate love
all night long, or should she thank him for a lovely time
and send him on his way? Guess what? There's no one
right answer to this question. It depends.

The wisdom behind that old bag of chestnuts that
decrees that a woman must never sleep with a man until
at least the third date, or possibly until he proposes or
even marries her — if she can hold out, that is — goes
back to the days when *men* were the ones who were supposed to want sex and women . . . were not. According to
the roles society gave us to play, men were out to score as
many notches on their bedposts as they could, and "nice
girls" didn't. Women were not only thought of as the
prey — breathless rabbits trying to outwit the clever
hawks (the men) who pursued them — they often
thought of themselves that way, too. Some still do.

However, a good number of modern-day gals are
much more proactive when it comes to sex than their pre-
decessors. Like men, many have learned that there *is* such
a thing as casual sex. They have also finally figured out
something that men have known all along: you can separate sex from love and still have a marvelous time. So,
let's get back to Claudia and Terrence.

If Claudia wants to take Terrence upstairs and dance
the horizontal mambo with him 'til the cows come home,
provided she's got ample protection, there's no reason for

her not to, nor should she feel badly about herself in the light of dawn. There's no reason to worry that she's "easy," or that anyone else is going to think about her in that way, either. If all she wants is sex and that's all Terrence wants as well, then as long as they treat each other with mutual respect, as adults they have every right to follow their inclination.

Aha! you're saying, *but what if Claudia wants more? What if she wants a relationship? She's ruined her chances, right?* Wrong again. Men love women who love sex. Men want to be with women who want to be with them. This can work—as long as Claudia doesn't fall into the trap of making the assumption that doing the deed suddenly launches the relationship toward the commitment department (tenth floor, next to the bridal registry and fine crystal). One act of sex does not a boyfriend/girlfriend unit make. Claudia is still Claudia, and Terrence is still Terrence. They are still a long way from becoming a couple.

If Claudia can keep her perspective intact, knowing that having Terrence make love to her does not necessarily mean that Terrence is *in love* with her—though that, too, is possible—it's perfectly viable for them to continue to date each other, sleep with each other, and just see where the road takes them. However, while some people can walk this line with "nookie" stops along the way and suffer no fallout, others cannot. Claudia is the only one who knows her own mind—and you are the only one who knows yours. If you don't think you can handle sex without love, don't do it. If you bring home a date and sleep with him, then the next day decide that perhaps you should pull back, that's fine, too.

Deciding at what point you should or shouldn't be having sex is entirely up to you. The only person you need to please, and ultimately, the only one you have to answer to, is yourself. Just listen to what Tamara, a twenty-three-year-old designer, has to say on the subject. "My boyfriend Shawn and I have been together for two years now, and we slept together on our very first date," she confesses. "The sex was great, and I knew that we were going to see each other again. He'd had a taste and he liked it. I was fairly certain that he'd be back for more. It's no big deal sleeping with a man right away. Maybe it was like that a bazillion years ago, but not now. Most guys are grateful to be getting sex at all," she adds with a laugh. "They're not going to be like, *Been there, done that, bye-bye now.* Yes, there are men who have that mentality, but no one worthwhile."

Remember, none of this is etched in stone. Listen to your feelings and trust them. Whatever you decide will ultimately be right for you. And if you feel you've made a mistake along the way, don't beat yourself up over it, just try to learn from it and move on.

"I love you" and other no-nos

Over the centuries, an intricate dating etiquette has developed between men and women, dictating that the male must take the dominant role while the female remains passive.

But it takes two to dance this tango. Many women, if not at first happy to comply, buckled under at last out of fear of the alternative. Over eons of programming, they began to embrace this regime as right and good. Ironically, these same women who'd handed over their autonomy found a subtle way to "get even." They began to regard men as inferior, insensitive creatures, and in so doing, gave themselves permission to manipulate them. They found a way to dehumanize men as they felt they'd been dehumanized, in effect turning the tables on their oppressors.

Unfortunately, as hard as some of us have fought to gain back ground, champions of the status quo insist on continuing the tradition. And they are the ones telling us that we're still not supposed to upset the applecart, especially in the world of relationships. Women, we're warned, must never do the asking about anything of consequence, and even more important, must never be the first to say, "I love you."

The reasoning behind this code is that words are power; initiative is power; and men won't tolerate having that power usurped. When women "go first," we're throwing the order of the universe out of whack. If we commit this affront to men's egos, they will retaliate by rejecting us. And it's true that some of them will. Not all men are evolved. Not all men are secure enough with themselves to view this kind of honesty as anything other than a challenge that must be dealt with and crushed.

However, the time has come when a lot of people have recognized this pattern of behavior for what it is and have said that enough is enough. Women who don't want to be ruled or to have to manipulate to get what they want are taking a stand, and thankfully, there are just as many guys out there who not only appreciate this attitude, they welcome it. It turns out that plenty of men want honesty as much as women do. They want to be with someone who is self-sufficient and can speak her mind. They don't want to have to make all the decisions and suffer all the consequences.

In taking back power over our own actions, women are not forcing men to give in to us. We are not depriving them of something that intrinsically belongs to them. We are reclaiming what is ours, reinstating our voice, and as a result, making ourselves responsible for the decisions we make. By saying, "Only I get to choose for me," not only do we allow both parties to approach issues of love and commitment on a level playing field, we can climb out from under the thumb of convention and quit blaming men for everything that goes wrong in our lives. We allow ourselves to stop being victims and to stop seeing men as victimizers. We can put an end to using sub-terfuge to get what we want, and deal honestly instead.

When this revelation finally came to Delia, it changed her entire attitude about men and put her on the road to a much more satisfying love life. "Whenever I was with a man, I spent so much of my time censoring my feelings and monitoring my actions that I could never enjoy myself," she admits. "I'd be angry at my lover because he wasn't giving me what I wanted. And I'd be angry at myself because I wasn't able to tell him what I wanted. All of the women who had been my role models had made it clear that you had to 'guide' men along, to play with their heads to get them to perform for you—to deliver. That was supposed to be all right. But it never felt all right to me.

"Every time I'd be working those wiles, there'd be this nagging in my head, my conscience probably, saying, *Why not just tell this guy the truth? Tell him how you feel. Tell him what you want.* But for the longest while, I couldn't bring myself to do it. I was afraid that if I told a man that I cared about him, he wouldn't find me desirable any-more. It got to be that whenever I had a date, I had to pack a roll of antacids in my purse. All this internal wran-gling had my stomach tied up in knots."

Finally, Delia's conscience overcame her years of social conditioning. "I'd been dating Robert for almost three months and I had fallen for him—hard," she recounts. "I was going through my usual turmoil. I want-ed to tell him so badly that I loved him, but he hadn't said it first, so that wasn't allowed. I'd never felt so com-fortable with a man, so safe, so happy. I had all these emotions and nowhere to put them. I felt like I was going to explode. One night, over dinner, I looked into Robert's eyes and in that instant realized that I had to tell him.

"When you really love someone, you don't want to play them, you want them to know how you feel. It was the hardest thing I've ever done. But the minute the words had crossed my lips, I knew it was right. I felt strong, liberated. My stomachache evaporated. I can't say I wasn't dying to know how what he'd say, but even while most of me was on the edge of my seat waiting for his response, some part of my psyche was giving that little, *You go, girl!* cheer."

Delia reports that Robert's reaction to her emotional declaration was a positive one. "I guess I'd had good instincts about him from the beginning," she concludes. "Maybe it took finding 'a keeper' to make me open up that way in the first place, but I'd like to think that it would have happened in any event. By being able to be honest and uninhibited with my feelings for the first time, I've finally achieved real intimacy with a man. This man knows the real me, not just some pretend woman who's always hiding from the truth. I tell him when he pleases me, I tell him when he pisses me off, I tell him when I'm happy and let him console me when I'm down."

Another argument for putting your cards on the table sooner rather than later is that some guys just can't stand having to be the first to ante up. Let's face it, there are times when getting a man to say "I love you" can be harder than pulling teeth. Being the first to utter those three little words is always a risk. What if the object of your affections doesn't feel the same way you do? If the passion is returned, we're elated; if not, we're crushed. Traditionally, men have been trained to take casual rejection a lot better than women. Maybe that's why we think of them as being so thick-skinned. But when it comes to baring their souls, these tough guys are often terrified. Men don't like to lose, especially when it involves something in which they've made a deep emotional investment, and they may drag their heels for as long as they can before taking the leap.

If you've ever found yourself in a situation in which you know that the man you're dating cares about you but is holding back from telling you his feelings out of fear, "going first" can give your lover the safety net he needs to move ahead. He's a lot more likely to swing out on the trapeze if he already knows he's not going to be splattered across the pavement for his efforts. When the man responds to your "I love you" with an "I love you, too," as long as he's sincere, not only does it count, it will make saying it the next time that much easier for him.

This also holds true in regard to those of you who are wondering whether or not it's a good idea for you to be the first to broach the topics of marriage, living together, and having children.

Listen to what Teresa, a now happily married woman, has to say on the subject: "If I had waited for Stan to tell me he loved me first, I'd probably still be waiting. Stan is a great guy, and as far as I'm concerned, the sun rises and sets on him. He's incredibly thoughtful and romantic, and we've got tons in common intellectually. His sense of humor is outrageous, and sexually, he's dynamite. We knew we were made for each other almost from the very beginning, but Stan is one of those people who had a problem with commitment. Well, maybe commitment isn't the right word—change would probably be more accurate. When it came to relationships, he would get used to having things a certain way. Things would go along, he'd get comfortable, and that was enough for him. But it wasn't enough for me, and I was always up front about it—not in a judgmental way. I'd just let him know what I wanted and told him how I felt about things."

After they had been going out for a couple of months, Teresa knew that she was ready for an exclusive relationship, and she hoped Stan felt the same. "I cared about him an awful lot by then. I didn't want to see anybody else, and I didn't want him to see other people, either. That's where my head was at. If he wasn't comfortable with it, then I'd have two choices: I could continue the relationship knowing that I had a lot more to lose than he did, or I could walk away. But whatever happened, I was the captain of my own ship and I would have no one to blame but myself if I decided to stay the course."

Teresa reports that Stan didn't leap on the bandwagon immediately. "He'd been a dyed-in-the-wool bachelor for quite a while and he was set in his ways. It wasn't that he wanted to see anyone else, it was more the idea that he wouldn't be able to that he couldn't come to grips with. I couldn't expect him to jump in with both feet on my say-so," Teresa explains, "but what I could and did do was to set a time limit. I let him know I understood how big a step this was for him, so I told him he could have a month to think it over. After that, if he still didn't feel right about it, we could just move on.

"I've got to stress here that this wasn't just some game I was playing. I meant it. It would have hurt like hell, but when that month was up, I would have picked up my marbles and gone home." When the time came, Stan agreed to an exclusive relationship, not because he'd been tricked into it, but because he really wanted to be with Teresa and in order to do that, he would have to honor her terms.

In every subsequent phase of their union, when it came to making decisions, the pattern was pretty much the same. "It just so happened that I knew what I wanted first," says Teresa. "After we'd been dating six months, I brought up the subject of our getting a place together. He took some time to think it over. We found an apartment. We moved in. After a year came 'the big one'—marriage.

Again, I put a time limit on it. I really loved him, but I didn't feel right about having kids outside marriage. I wanted the ceremony. I wanted us to stand up in front of all of our friends and before God and say, 'This is it.' And it turns out, Stan wanted that, too. Yes, I did let him know that I had marriage on my mind, but Stan did the proposing, ring from Tiffany's, bended knee and all."

By explaining her needs clearly and by setting limits, Teresa was able to satisfy her relationship requirements without damage to Stan's ego. At no time did she make false threats in order to force his hand. The reason Teresa succeeded was that she was willing to put her money where her mouth was. She stood by every bargain she made, and left Stan free to decide for himself whether or not he wanted to take her up on it.

Like the rules, the anti-rules aren't for everybody, but don't let that stop you from using them, because for every man living with nineteenth-century blinders on who thinks a woman's place is two steps to the rear, there's another looking toward the next millennium who wants a partner who can not only keep up with his stride, but set the pace, as well.

So go ahead, set your limits, tell him "I love you," ask him to dance, pick up the occasional check, and have sex if you want to. All you'll be doing is taking your best shot at love. It's time to stop trusting your destiny to the defunct, moth-eaten dogma you dug out of your grandmother's trunk. Even if these anti-rules don't work out every time, at least you won't feel like some schizophrenic "Who do I have to be to be loved?" basket case when you look at yourself in the mirror. You'll just be you—and with a man or without one, there's nothing wrong with that!

PART THREE

The Sexual (R)evolution

CHAPTER 9

Sex in the Dark Ages

EVEN TODAY, SEXUALLY ASSERTIVE women often find themselves confronted with lots of negative feedback—both from their peers and from insecure men. The source of this friction probably dates back to the times when premarital sex was a definite no-no—especially for women. In an era when marriage or spinsterhood were your only options, the "Why should he buy the cow if he can get the milk for free?" argument was a lot more persuasive. Apart from the moral censure "oversexed" women faced, there was also the issue an "easy" woman faced in catching a husband. It seemed that men certainly didn't mind corrupting a girl, but they would take no part in marrying the ones who were corruptible, or worse yet, had been corrupted by someone else.

God forbid that a woman actually consummated her passions before she took her vows. Should anyone find out that a man had taken a sleigh ride through her field of pure, driven snow, she could expect to be cast aside as damaged goods. When a man came to the party, he wanted a whole, new slice of pizza, pristine and perfect, to be set before him. Last night's leftovers, or a pie that someone had already picked the pepperoni off, were not acceptable. And woe to the woman who'd had her pepperoni plucked!

Of course, one main reason for women not having sex outside of marriage was the possibility of becoming

pregnant. Even today, in many faiths, the religious affili-
ation of the child is passed down through the mother's
line. Why? It's simple. You always know who the mother
is, but the dad can be anybody. Historically, fathers
wanted to be certain that sons who inherited property
were sprung from their own loins—not the milkman's.

Sadly, somewhere in this process of ensuring the puri-
ty of male bloodlines, it was decreed that females were
not allowed to own land, nor had they any rights of succession, thus effectively cutting them off from any viable
means of self-sufficiency. Heirs had to be male. Sons got
the goods, daughters got the shaft. Even a distant
cousin—as long as he was a man—took precedence over
direct female descendants. (It's the stuff Jane Austen's
work is made of.)

But back in an age that many modern men think best
forgotten, there were a lot of places in the world where
women held real power. The earth was mother and the
wisdom of females was regarded as both profound and
divine. But at some point, a group of disgruntled males,
probably high on mead and testosterone poisoning,
decided that the ways of women were too vague and all-
encompassing. Rather than seeing themselves as a small
part of a larger universe, they wanted the universe to
revolve around them. They wanted to own things, to control things, to mark their territory.

From the moment that the Judeo-Christian patriarchy
yanked the rug out from under the Goddess and cast her
children (women) into bondage, there's been a whole laundry list of things that suddenly became the sole province of
men, and heaven help the woman who dared try to
express herself in a way that was considered a threat to the
male domain. In the new order, men went to work, women
stayed home. Men spoke their minds, women listened and
obeyed. Men owned property, women *were* property.

Those females who practiced ancient ways of healing were tried as witches and burned at the stake. Those who behaved in a manner deemed too aggressive, who pursued men openly or, worse, casually, were labeled with scarlet letters and made outcasts in their communities. Women who had the temerity to behave in ways that were considered "masculine" always came to bad ends. They died miserable, lonely deaths and their children lived to pay for their sins. From the Bible to Joan of Arc, *Madame Bovary* to *Anna Karenina*, our literature is filled with examples of women who crossed the line and paid the price.

• • •

Once, long ago, there was a girl named Addie. Now some might say that she was an ordinary girl; her father, a widower, had little property to speak of other than the small inn he ran, so she was without a dowry; she could neither play the lute nor trip the fashionable dances of the court; she was not schooled in wit or artifice, and her knowledge of the arts, mathematics, physics, and philosophy were limited to what little she'd picked up from the occasional educated travelers who stopped for the night at her father's public house while on their way to some infinitely more interesting location. So, in those respects, one might have called Addie plain. But Addie had a huge heart and a sound body. She could outrun any boy in the village and carry an even load with her older brother, Seth, who was almost twice her size.

As to her face, well, Addie was pretty. She did not possess the fine, cold elegance of porcelain or crystal. No, her beauty was something warm and living, something rooted in earth but reaching toward heaven like a blooming tree. She was slow to anger, quick to laugh, and when she sang, more than once the fairies nearly overstayed the dawn to catch one last sweet note of her lilting voice.

As she grew older, her father fretted more and more about Addie's prospects. With no mother to guide her, no dowry to attract a suitable husband, and the way she carried on—so like a boy—what was to become of her once he was gone? Though he loved his son, he knew that Seth's head might as well have been filled with straw as the brains God gave him. Too often in the morning he would find the lad lying in a drunken stupor, his chores done by Addie along with her own. What a pity that he couldn't leave the inn to Addie so that her future and some small income might be assured! But the laws of the land forbade women from owning property, so all the innkeeper could do was make Seth his heir, charge him to take care of his sister . . . and hope for the best.

As it happened, one day a caravan of four wagons, laden with sumptuous, exotic goods gathered from every corner of the globe, pulled into the courtyard of the inn. At the head of the procession was an ornately gilded coach, from which alighted a wealthy merchant who in age was well past the bloom of youth, but still young enough to have some sap flowing through his veins.

"Innkeeper!" he barked at the top of his lungs. The innkeeper, who had been up in the hayloft at the time the wagons arrived, was climbing down the steep ladder with as much speed as his aching limbs could muster, when he heard the stranger bellow, "In the name of hell's three-headed dog, can't a man get any service here?"

Before her father could stop her, Addie sailed up to the merchant under a full head of steam and planted herself directly in his path. "Greetings, sir," she said, dropping him a curtsy more in challenge than in deference. "We are happy to serve all *civil* gentlemen who stop here."

"Addie!" her father called out, alarmed.

The merchant looked Addie up and down, contemplating the strange, bold creature who barred his path. Now, this fellow was very shrewd and he had a keen talent for sizing up the hidden value of something less discerning eyes might overlook, and in Addie he knew he had found an untapped source of treasure. *Why, cleaned up and tutored in more gentle ways*, he thought to himself, *this girl would make a most agreeable wife for any man . . . and in view of her present circumstances*, he noted, making a brief mental assessment of the inn and of its occupants, *she could be got for a song . . .*

By then, the innkeeper, who had worked himself into a fearful state, tottered up to the merchant and interjected, "You must forgive my child for being so forward," he apologized. "She is unused to the company of genteel folk such as yourself and . . ."

But here the merchant cut him off. "Nonsense," he replied, "your daughter is quite right. It is *I* who owe *you* a thousand apologies."

"Sir? I . . ." the flabbergasted innkeeper began to protest, but the merchant merely continued.

"Please pardon my abrupt behavior. We have traveled far this day and I fear that I am out of sorts. Perhaps the hospitality of your fine establishment can restore my better humor and along with it my manners." Next, he turned to Addie, fixed her with a broad smile, and said, "Dearest lady, if I am forgiven, will you accompany me inside and tell a reformed blackguard where he might wash the dirt of a thousand roads from his person and revive himself with food and drink?"

"It would be my pleasure," said Addie. "This way, if you please."

The merchant was not the only member of the entourage to be struck by Addie's brave spirit and beauty. From his perch on the last wagon, a dark-haired youth named Rafael had watched her every move, every gesture, taking in each expression that worked across her intelligent face and savoring like a starving man the sweet, steady tones that flowed across her lips.

"Rafael," the merchant called out in a manner a shade too hearty to ring true, "please help this admirable fellow tend to the horses, then guard the goods." Addressing the other drivers in the same cheery fashion, he summoned them to join him inside.

Rafael, who was a cunning youth, could see what his master was after, and if things ran their usual course, he knew it would just be a matter of time before he prevailed. *On the other hand*, he considered, *this girl has a mind of her own; perhaps she will beat him at his game.*

Rafael and the innkeeper had their hands full for quite some time. As they got the last horse into its stall, curried, fed, and watered, a drowsy Seth appeared from the hayloft and muttered, "What a commotion. I could hardly sleep!" Then, smelling the aroma of stew and fresh-baked bread drifting across the courtyard, he climbed down and made his way to the kitchen in search of food. Resigned, the innkeeper rolled his eyes to heaven and shook his head. For his part, Rafael said nothing and continued with his chores.

When they had finished, the innkeeper said to him, "Come, lad, let's retire inside and I shall reward you for your efforts with a fine meal. My daughter Addie may be a bit of a hellion, but she's a fine cook." But Rafael declined, explaining that he must polish the tack and stay with the wagons until one of the other drivers returned. "Ah, right you are then," the old man replied, "I'll send one of them out directly"; then he left the barn.

Once inside the inn, he could barely believe the scene that unfolded before his eyes. At the long oak table sat the merchant and his comrades, and ensconced within the bosom of their company sat Seth! The merchant had his arm around him and was praising him and clapping him on the back. Noting the old man's return, he cried out in delight, "Sir, what remarkable children you have! You are to be congratulated! Please join us, for I have a proposition to offer you, man to man, and it will not do to have you standing."

Incredulous, the innkeeper did as the merchant requested and sat down at the table. "Your son," the merchant began, "is a fine, intelligent youth, and I believe he shows great promise. Would you consider letting him accompany me on a brief journey? We are headed for a spice market that is but a week's travel from here. I believe that in that time I should be able to test his mettle and discern if he has the potential I am seeking for a junior partner." At that point, Addie nearly dropped the platter of meat she was carrying to the table, but somehow managed to regain her composure.

Needless to say, the innkeeper was dumbfounded. "I hardly know what to say, sir. But if you took my Seth on the road, who would help me at the inn?"

"Your daughter seems quite capable," he replied offhandedly, readying himself for the kill. "In fact, I have taken something of a shine to her, and since I am a widower, I thought that upon my return, with your permission, I might take her for my wife."

"Well, I really don't know . . ." the innkeeper spluttered.

"No need to decide now," the merchant went on smoothly.

"But the inn, I . . ." the innkeeper tried to object, thinking less of the loss of Addie than of Seth, who was pretty much of a loss anyway.

"If you'd like, I can leave Rafael behind to help while your son accompanies me on the road."

"Well, it's . . ."

"Settled, then," the merchant concluded. "And what do you think of that, my fine girl?" he turned to ask Addie. But she had slipped out of the room and fled to the kitchen.

"Gone to check the venison, I expect," the unnerved innkeeper suggested weakly, then excused himself and went to join his daughter.

"Addie, did you hear what the man said?"

"Yes, father," she replied, not able to bring herself to turn and face him.

"Addie, an offer like this comes but once in a lifetime for a dowerless girl such as yourself. You will be a fine lady and live in a fine house with servants to do your bidding. You shall neither hunger nor want for anything."

But Addie knew that if she were to marry this man, she would spend the rest of her life hungering, for the merchant's smile left her heart unmoved and his touch chilled the very blood in her veins. Addie was a passionate girl. Faced with the prospect of a life totally devoid of passion, she felt her head begin to swim, and yet her father talked on.

"I have been so worried what was to become of you — both of you — and now you shall be taken care of. Knowing this, I can go to my grave in peace."

"Dear father," Addie beseeched him, "do not speak of dying. How can I leave you behind? Who would look after you?"

"I can sell the inn and take some small rooms in town," he told her. "There will be enough to see me through." Addie shook her head, tears of sorrow and frustration stinging her eyes and running down her cheeks. "Now, Addie," her father said, "haven't I always taken care of you?" Addie nodded. "Then you must obey my wishes in this matter. Really it is for the best." Though her heart was filled with dread, she nodded again.

"Now, take a plate of food and some bread out to that boy in the stable," the innkeeper told her gently. "He must be famished."

Numbly, Addie ladled some stew into a bowl and pulled a fresh loaf from the hearth, then went to bring them to Rafael. He took them from her hands gratefully, but he could see by the look on Addie's face that the merchant had already played his hand.

"He wants to marry you, doesn't he?" remarked Rafael bitterly.

Addie looked into his face, and for the first time in her life, saw with the eyes of a woman's love; her heart, which had been numb, now ached. "Yes," she answered. "It has been arranged. He is taking my brother with him on the road to bring him into the business. You are to stay behind to help my father. And when the caravan returns . . .when the caravan returns . . ." but she could not bring herself to speak the words.

"You must marry him," said Rafael.

Filled with rueful anger, Addie cried aloud, "Curse me that I was born a woman and cannot choose my own fate!"

"But had you not been born a woman," Rafael replied, "then I would not love you."

"Nor I you," she said, taking his hand and placing it upon her breast. "And if I am doomed to live a life without love, then we must love each other now."

"But Addie," he protested, "this cannot be. I am less than nothing and could never marry you. Your father would never consent, and bless me if he wouldn't be right!"

"Don't you want me?" she demanded, her eyes welling again with tears.

"You know that I do," he told her, and, unable to control his desire any longer, he pulled her into his arms and kissed her deeply.

"Come on," she said, taking him by the hand. Together, they climbed the ladder to the hayloft. Addie slipped out of her shift, took the ribbon from her hair, and lay down hidden from view in the straw. Rafael removed his own clothes and lay down beside her. Tentatively at first, they explored each other's bodies. Addie, shivering from the cold, pressed herself snugly against Rafael's chest. Soon, their soft moans wove together in the night, ecstasy rocking through their bodies like a full-force gale, until all at once and in unison, they succumbed to their joy. Cradled in each other's arms, the two then fell asleep.

In the morning when Rafael woke, Addie was nowhere to be found. For a moment, he thought perhaps he'd dreamed the whole thing, but there, tangled in the straw, was Addie's hair ribbon. Quickly, Rafael dressed, grabbed the ribbon and secreted it away in a pocket, then carefully turned the straw to destroy any evidence of the previous evening's activities. He had just completed his task when he heard the merchant's voice bellowing to him from the courtyard.

"Rafael, you worthless spawn of a donkey! Where are you?"

"Here," he called, rushing to attend his master's request.

"Rafael, ready the wagons," the merchant command-ed; then, pointing to Seth, who stood next to him grin-ning smugly, he continued, "I shall be taking this admirable fellow along as my . . . er, um . . . apprentice, on this journey and have contracted with the innkeeper that you should stay behind in his absence and take up his duties."

"As you wish," Rafael replied, trying to appear put out.

"Seth," said the merchant, "would you be so kind as to go back into the inn and fetch my small chest? I appear to have left it behind."

"Certainly," fawned the youth, and ran to fetch the thing.

"Rafael," intoned the merchant in a grave tone, "come here." When the boy stood within a whisper's distance, he went on, "I am leaving some rather valuable merchandise behind, if you catch my meaning."

"The girl?" Rafael inquired.

"I see you are a bright boy, after all," the merchant allowed. "Keep an eye on her for me, as I intend to marry her upon my return. Do a good job and there'll be a gold piece in it for your trouble."

"You can rely on me, sir," replied the youth, whose heart was now racing. By the end of the morning, the caravan was ready to leave. Seth took up Rafael's seat on the last wagon, eager for the journey to begin. Until then, Addie had made no appearance. Showing up at the last possible moment, she handed the merchant a basket of provisions for the road and bid him a curt farewell, but he only smiled, thinking that he'd won his prize. "Farewell, dear lady," he said, ignoring her ill humor; "in a fortnight's time we begin our lives anew."

From the doorway, the innkeeper watched the tense exchange, hoping that in time, Addie would come to appreciate her good fortune and learn to love this man who was to be her husband. *It's really for the best*, he told himself, then turned and retreated inside the inn.

A moment later, the courtyard was deserted, except for Addie and Rafael. "Boy," she called to him, "the hour is late and we have many chores to do before the end of day. Come with me and I will acquaint you with your duties."

"Yes, miss," he replied deferentially. "Lead the way." And lead the way she did, not to the barn, the wellspring, or the vegetable gardens, but out into the meadow, across one field and the next, until they reached a meadow filled

with blooming heather, where they fell into each other's
arms once more, then sank onto the flowering earth to
kiss, caress, and make love until the prospect of their
inevitable parting was washed, for a time at least, from
their minds.

Each day, their chores completed, the lovers continued
to meet in this place, taking and giving pleasure and
falling deeper and deeper in love. But too soon, the
appointed time passed and the merchant returned. As the
caravan pulled into the courtyard, Addie felt as if a knife
had been driven through her heart. The thought of losing
Rafael and being forced to let a man for whom she felt
nothing touch and use her body sickened her, but she
was trapped. She could not abandon her obligation to her
father; if it was his wish that she marry this man, then
marry him she must.

From the moment the merchant came back, Rafael
was nearly silent, keeping his conversation to a minimum for fear his emotions would betray him. His countenance took on a gray pallor, and his eyes, once so full
of light, filled with black despair. On the evening before
the wedding, he could no longer tolerate his sorrow, and
taking with him no more than the clothing on his back,
he bolted, blind with anguish, out of the barn and over
the fields.

But his departure did not go unnoticed. Addie, who
had not slept since the caravan's return, spied her lover
as he fled, and as she watched him running out of her life
forever, a small flame of her former self was renewed.
Without a thought of consequence, she crept silently out
of her bedchamber and followed him into the night. She
knew where he was going, even if he did not, and sometime later, weary and out of breath, her nightdress torn to
shreds, she found him in their secret place. He had
thrown himself on the ground and lay there, weeping.

Addie fell to her knees, nestling her lover's head in her bosom. In a moment, their need overtook them, and that was their undoing.

For the merchant, observant as he was, had seen from the moment of his return that something was amiss. He could tell, by the wooden way in which Addie moved through her day as if she were a puppet, that the fine thing he prized in her was lost. But what had happened? Looking about and studying the situation, he perceived that Rafael, too, walked around as if he were made of stone. The answer was all too clear.

Now, the merchant was a spiteful man, who resented being bested in any way, so this debacle cut him to the quick, and he vowed revenge. He no longer had any intention of marrying Addie, but he would ruin her if he could. He kept up the charade most admirably, all the while keeping his eyes on the lovers, waiting for the time when he could get back a little of his own, and soon enough, the moment came.

Donning a dark cloak, he slipped out stealthily into the night and trailed Addie to her assignation. Though the sight of the lovers locked in their carnal embrace choked him with jealousy and rage, he held his tongue. Rather than rush upon them and end them on the spot, he now had the tools he needed to build for them a lifetime of anguish and despair. A cruel smile turned up the corner of his lip as he thought of the vengeance he would soon wreak upon the luckless pair.

Sometime before dawn, Addie rose and, placing one last kiss on her lover's brow, headed back to the inn to prepare herself for the wedding. As the morning wore on, all went as planned. The inn bustled with activity and the innkeeper whistled happily, thinking of how far his children had come up in the world and how much further they might yet climb. The innkeeper could see that the merchant doted on Addie, and much to his surprise and delight, he also seemed well-pleased with Seth's progress and made a show of complimenting him on his abilities.

"Odd," the merchant remarked to Seth as the hour of the wedding approached, "I can't seem to find that rascal Rafael anywhere. Well, no matter, he'll turn up sooner or later."

At noon, the party headed for the church and made ready for the wedding ceremony. All the townsfolk had turned up for the occasion, and there was great hubbub and excitement in the air. The priest began the ceremony, charging the bride and groom with their usual duties, and went on without incident until he reached that portion of the service in which he must ask the company if anyone knew of any reason why the couple who stood before him should not be wed.

It was then that the merchant spoke up. "I cannot marry this woman," he stated coldly. For a minute, Addie could not believe her ears. She felt like someone about to be hanged who receives last-minute clemency—but her relief was to be short-lived.

"What's this all about?" the innkeeper demanded. "What are you saying?"

"What I'm saying is that your daughter is no virgin. She is no better than a harlot. I've have seen her lying with her lover like a bitch in heat, and I will have none of her."

"How dare you, sir!" the innkeeper shouted, beside himself with rage and fury.

"My charges are not unfounded," the merchant pressed on mercilessly. He turned toward the door at the back of the church, where two of his caravan drivers now entered with Rafael, bloody and beaten, pinned between them. "There is her lover!" he spat. "A worthless traveler. A gypsy. I believe your daughter's struck a perfect bargain," he sneered at the innkeeper, "a whore for a whore's son . . . and as for your own heir, a two-year-old could outwit him in a trade. He hasn't the cunning God gave a leather boot." And with that, the merchant turned on his heel, stormed out of the church, and was never seen again.

For a moment, Addie stood ashen-faced and frozen at the altar; then, taking her faltering father by the arm, she walked back down the aisle to a chorus of taunts and jeers from the townspeople. Seth, not knowing what else to do, went after them, and picking the unconscious Rafael up in his arms, carried him back to the inn.

In the days that followed, the innkeeper's health failed him. In less than a week, he was dead. Rafael woke up eventually, but his mind and body were shattered, and Addie's life became a waking nightmare, until one day, before anyone could stop him, Rafael raced out into the road and was killed by a speeding coach.

Without their father to run it, the inn fell into disrepair, but it hardly mattered since no customers had crossed the threshold since the day of the wedding. Seth, who had no heart for cruelty and no mind for reality, became a drunkard, begging for copper pennies in the town and telling to all who'd listen the story of his glorious days as a traveling merchant. And Addie? Some months after the death of Rafael she disappeared, and though her legend lived on for generations as a warning to young girls of the consequences of allowing themselves to fall into sin, debauchery, and temptation, she was never heard from again.

● ● ●

To add insult to injury, the ancient logic that decreed that both you and your betrothed were supposed to march to your marriage beds as virgins always had a tacit double standard attached: men were never required to be as pure as women. If a groom had sown a few wild oats, the fact was generally acknowledged with a complicit or even congratulatory "boys will be boys" wink from his cohorts as he walked up the aisle. Since there's technically no way to prove the "is he or isn't he?" virgin status of a man, you just had to take his word for it.

Now, this custom of turning a blind eye to male dalliance may have stemmed in part from fatalism. Men have been marching off to wars for as long as anyone can remember, and their thinking may have been, *If I'm going to die, I might as well get some first. After all, even condemned prisoners are fed a last meal before they go to the executioner's block, right?*

Well, whatever the root of the rationale, society's prevailing standard was to accept that men had certain "manly" needs to which they were slaves, and that sometimes, in the rashness of youthful impetuosity, even the best of them lost control. And while this type of behavior wasn't ideal, women were taught that it was excusable—sort of like the beloved Uncle George who went off on a bender from time to time. One simply brought him home, sobered him up, and pretended it had never happened.

For women, on the other hand, it was an entirely different story. As females, we weren't supposed to have strong sexual urges. Girls who showed any interest in sex outside of marriage were condemned for their aberrant inclinations. So, while a boy with a lusty nature might be considered high-spirited, a girl of the same breed was usually labeled a slut, or worse, a whore—and God forbid she bring a bastard into the world. That was the kiss of death.

By the nineteenth century, a few lucky ones were able to escape to cities like Chicago, New York, San Francisco, and even Paris to find work on the stage as chorus girls and actresses; the theater—which the general public often regarded as one step up, and not a very big one, from prostitution—being one of the few places where relaxed morality was accepted as part of life and women were as highly esteemed for scoring sexual conquests as their male contemporaries. The majority of young women, however, were either married off as quickly as possible to whatever man their parents could scrape up, usually from the bottom of the barrel; shipped off to a convent in the dead of night; or left to become social outcasts in their own communities, sneered and snickered at wherever they went. And usually, once you had a bad reputation—deserved or rumored—no amount of whitewashing could make it go away.

Good women were schooled to believe that their desires should lie dormant—like tulip bulbs—until after the wedding day. Once you had that ring on your finger, then and only then was sexual intercourse an option. Not that as a female you were expected or obligated to take much interest in it. Women were not responsible for their own pleasure, and women's pleasures were thought to be irrelevant, if they were thought of at all.

After the ceremony, it was the husband who became the formal gardener of our desires. It was up to him to nurture and cultivate our libidos for us. He was our sunshine, our fertilizer, and our watering can. Now, of course, there were many husbands who were tender, loving, and patient when it came to lovemaking, but when the flower beds blossomed, it was usually more to his benefit than the wife's. As a man, he had the marital right to plow the soil at his whim. If the wife enjoyed it, it was more often only by happy accident; if not, wifely duty demanded that she lie back and let him do his business. Talk about fertilizer . . .

Now, in this earlier, or what some call "simpler" time—as if to imply that simpler is better—when these two theoretical virgins got together, they both knew practically diddly about what it really took to make a marriage work, and this mutual ignorance was actually supposed to work for them. Supposedly, they would grow into their union, and learn about love along the way. But the big problem was that when you have nothing to measure your experience against, it might as well exist in a vacuum. Women who had married men who were unskilled, uncreative, lazy, or even destructive between the sheets had no basis for comparison. And though instinctively most of them must have known something was wrong, they could never put a name to it.

But with the advent of birth control and the suffragette movement, social attitudes began to shift. Women refused to be the "cow" any longer, or at least we made it clear that we were within our rights to see if a bull's stuff was up to snuff before we took him home on a permanent basis. As women made their way into the work force and financial constraints loosened, the necessity for the marriage contract eroded. Women no longer *needed* to be married to be considered useful, viable citizens, at least from an economic standpoint, and that opened the door for them to engage in sex outside of wedlock.

Thankfully, in many circles today, a sexually experienced woman is prized rather than condemned. A gal who knows how to enjoy herself *and* please her man is highly sought after, not shunned. We're seeing that men appreciate women who express honesty, creativity, and enthusiasm in bed much more than someone who makes them guess, fakes her pleasure, or just lies there like a slab of meat.

CHAPTER 10

Seduction and the Sex-Positive Woman

SHOULD A WOMAN TAKE CONTROL of seduction? Isn't the man supposed to make that first move? The answer to the first question is "Yes, if she wants to," and to the second, "It depends." Not every man wants to play caveman. Not all of them want to dominate and control (if they did, a lot of women who have lucrative careers dressing up in black leather and stiletto heels and brandishing riding crops would be out of business).

There are plenty of potential lovers who are more than willing to let you share turns in the driver's seat, and even some who'd love it if you took over completely. Again, no one set of behaviors is going to match up with every variable of individual likes and dislikes. Each man's ego is fine-tuned a little differently. Some are threatened by assertive women, some welcome them. When you size up a man to see what he's made of, if you find that he never wants you to be the one to introduce sex into the equation, you may decide that what he's made of is not for you.

Rather than focusing your energy on how to make sure *he's* happy in bed, you'll be a lot better off learning to express your own needs. Women who know what they want sexually, and aren't afraid to ask for it, stand a much

better chance of being satisfied. And it usually follows
that if you're happy in bed, your lover will be, too.
Nobody owns your sex life but you. Of course, your
lover's wishes are important, but you have every right to
follow your own inclinations and express your desires,
and this includes the right to be the one to initiate sex.

A Lovers' Timetable

Sexually speaking, those in the know are already savvy to
the fact that there's no set schedule when it comes to
being ready to make love in the context of a relationship.
It's an individual thing, which not only varies from person to person, but can change for one individual from situation to situation.

Sometimes you want hot sex; other times, you want to
hold off. (That's not to say that the sex won't be hot if you
wait, but not jumping the gun usually means you've got
something else on your agenda than just satisfying a
physical itch.) There are many women — possibly a
majority — who would just as soon not rush into physical
relations and prefer to really get to know a man before
going to bed with him.

Says Julia, "I have a reputation of playing hard to get,
but it really isn't the case. I don't have a 'three-date minimum' or anything like that.

"It's true that there are some guys who respond to my
playing it cool by seeming to want me that much more.
We're all susceptible to the thrill of anticipation, and
sometimes waiting does make the moment when you
finally do get together that much sweeter, but for me holding back sexually isn't about heightening his arousal or
making me more desirable, though I admit, it's sometimes
a happy by-product of the process. What I'm really after is
achieving a comfort level and establishing trust before I go

that next step. For me, a guy who isn't willing to take the time to do that is not someone I need to be with.

"Should the time come when I've been going out with a man long enough to know what he's about, and I feel that we've made the emotional and intellectual bond that I'm looking for, then I'll let him know that I want to have sex with him—in no uncertain terms. I like being graphic, even a little bit nasty, and I don't see any contradiction in that. I won't jump into bed with a man on the first date, but I'm not Miss Goody Two-Shoes by any stretch of the imagination."

Another woman who's in no hurry to hop in the sack when she first meets a man is Selena, who at twenty-three has decided that "an updated, old-fashioned approach," as she calls it, is what works best for her. "I actually *do* have a 'three-date minimum,'" she says, adding with a laugh, "but I've been known to stretch that to four, five, six, and even no go, depending on the man.

"Am I a tease? I don't think so. Not in the least. I'm just not into casual sex, no matter how attractive I find a man. I guess you could say that I'm just as prone to thinking with my lap instead of my head as the next person, but I'm just not comfortable with the idea of letting something purely physical cloud my judgment. I need to give myself time to sort out what my body is telling me from what will be good for me in the long run.

"Sure, waiting is tough sometimes, but for my peace of mind, it's necessary, and the majority of men I've dated have respected my point of view. They may have been ready for sex sooner than I was, but most were patient enough to wait until I was sure.

"But don't get me wrong. I would never talk myself into having sex with someone I don't click with physically, even if he's the most wonderful man on the planet in every other respect. Sexual attraction—chemistry—has got to be there. You can't force yourself to be attracted to someone you're not. I don't think you should even want to. That only hurts both of you in the end. You wind up feeling you're missing something, and he winds up feeling that he can't satisfy you.

"What happens once I am sure? It's really a subtle thing. In my mind, I actually see it like a gate that's been locked and I open it, or a wall that silently melts into mist. I've never had to tell someone, 'Okay, time to go for it!' They usually sense the change, and once they do, I like to let the man make the next move. I guess that's where the 'old-fashioned' part comes in, but I love to be seduced — dinner, dancing, wine, and hours of foreplay. Then to me, it's so much more than having sex, it's making love."

Kristen, a thirty-four-year-old massage therapist, has what some might call a New Age philosophy on sex. "Men are much more likely to get hung up on me sexually than I am on them," she admits. "As a result of what I do for a living, I'm very in tune with the human body. I've spent a lot of time studying sex practices from cultures all around the world. I've learned where the pleasure points are and how to stimulate them, how to enhance the sexual experience and take it to a much higher level. If a man trusts me, I can open him up to things he's never felt before that are so intensely erotic, he's usually blown away. Once they've gone through that, they almost always want more."

Kristen doesn't worry that if she initiates sex with a man it will ruin her chances of having a relationship with him. "That's just never happened," she states. "To me, every time I make love to a man, it's almost like a sacred ceremony. And while each experience resonates with its own rhythm, they all have a beginning, middle, and end. After I've had sex with a lover, I feel closure. If I choose to pursue other encounters with the same man, then so be it.

If not, then so be that, too. But who starts things off has never had any impact on whether my relationships sink or swim."

And at what point does Kristen introduce sex into the equation? "Sometimes immediately, sometimes down the road, sometimes never," she states. "When the right door opens, I walk through it. It's not like a certain number of grains of sand have to fall through the hourglass before sex becomes permissible. But then again," she points out, "I don't tend to think of time in as linear terms as most people do."

Many of the same men who appreciate having the pressure taken off them when it comes to asking women out are equally open to having the woman be the one to start the mating dance. Women who forge headlong into the sexual arena as an integral part of the mating process appreciate their own power, and men actually like the attention. Just knowing that a woman wants them on a sexual level can be a huge turn-on for them. Listen to what happened when Tony met Angela.

"I own my own business," Tony explains. "A garage. Angela started bringing her car to me about six months ago. It's an old Jaguar, a beauty, but it spends a lot of time in the shop. I couldn't help but notice Angela. Not only was she pretty, but there was just something about her that was fun and full of life. Whenever she stopped by, she always had a funny story to tell me, or a joke she'd heard. We got along great. But I had no idea she was interested in me, until one night . . .

"Angela had dropped off the car for some routine maintenance work. She was pretty fastidious about getting her tune-ups and oil changes. In fact, she kept a mileage log in the glove compartment, so she could keep track of when they were due. That afternoon, she called me up and asked if I could do her a couple of favors. She told me she'd forgotten to mark the mileage entry in the log and asked if I wouldn't mind jotting down the numbers. I told her that was no problem. Then she asked me if I could drop the car off at her house when the shop closed. She said she'd be happy to drive me back to pick up my car. This wasn't anything out of the ordinary. We did it fairly often for our regular customers. I told her I could be over to her place by around seven-thirty. She thanked me and hung up. I think it was around three o'clock at the time.

"After I'd finished changing the oil, I went and washed up. Then I popped open the glove compartment and pulled out the mileage log. Stuck dead in the middle of it was a medium-sized manila envelope with my name printed on it and the word 'Personal.' I started to record the mileage when I realized she hadn't forgotten to record it at all—there was her entry in black and white. Of course, I was dying of curiosity. I stuck the envelope in the pocket of my coveralls and went into the office for some privacy. After locking the door behind me, I tore it open and emptied the contents on my desk. Inside was a house key, a condom . . . and a pair of panties. I stuffed them back into the envelope and put it in my pocket again. Whew! Nothing like that had ever happened to me before.

"Needless to say, I was a wreck for the rest of the afternoon. I couldn't concentrate on anything, so I pretended to go over parts catalogues. Around seven, we closed up shop. I changed out of my work clothes, then walked over to Angela's Jag and got in. When I went to put the car in gear, my hand was shaking. I drove to her house in what felt like a dream and parked the car in her driveway. I took the key she'd given me and put it in the front door. The lock turned. When I stepped inside, she was waiting for me.

"She said, 'Glad you could make it,' and then she gave me a kiss that practically curled my toes. She asked me to follow her upstairs. By the time we got to the bedroom, my goose was cooked. As far as I was concerned, she could have done anything she wanted . . . and she did.

"The next morning—*late* the next morning—I woke up. I could hear Angela downstairs. I found my pants, put them on, and joined her in the kitchen. She was drinking coffee, reading the paper. 'Do you need a lift to work?' she asked. At that point I told her maybe I should blow off work and we could spend the day together . . . exploring. To my surprise, she said she was busy. She was as nice as she could be about it, but she told me she was driving up to see her mom for a few days. She was leaving that afternoon and couldn't change her plans. To say I was disappointed was an understatement, but what could I do? I went back upstairs, took a shower, got dressed, and let her drive me to work.

"As I was getting out of the car, she leaned over and gave me another one of those toe-curling kisses. Then she pulled those same panties out of her purse, handed them to me, and told me she'd call me when she got back. She was all I could think about for the next few days. I wanted to be with her again so bad it hurt. Finally, I couldn't take it any more. I broke down and left a message on her answering machine. She called me that night from her mom's house. 'I was wondering how long it would take you,' she teased. But I was in heaven just hearing her voice.

"You know, I've spent all of my life doing the chasing and I never thought that I'd be the one to get caught. Angela let me know how much she liked having me around, and for more than just sex, but she always made it clear that she had her own life and that it wasn't just suddenly going to stop now that she'd met me. I was just glad to be able to be a part of it.

"We've been together for almost ten years now. And I still get a big kick out if it when she meets me at the door and gives me one of her special kisses. I don't care how other men live their lives, I know I'm one hell of a lucky guy."

Angela was a woman who knew what she wanted and went after it. She wasn't afraid to make sexual demands, nor did she worry that by showing her lover what she wanted, she would damage his ego. But most important, her forthright bedside manner carried over into other aspects of her life as well. By living as she pleased, and seeing her lover when she wanted, she didn't tie her life down to suit his schedule, and so he learned to appreciate the time they spent together even more. Not all men could handle this, but Tony knew a good thing when he saw it, and was secure enough in his own masculinity to go with the flow.

Julia, Selena, Kristen, and Angela each have very different styles and attitudes when it comes to sex, but they all have one thing in common: they decide when or whether they're going to sleep with a man. There's nothing wrong with taking charge when it comes to love, and it's perfectly acceptable to have sex in other contexts than deep emotional commitment. It's up to each and every one of us to decide what we want and what makes us comfortable, and if letting the man make the first move is what works for you, that's all right, too. By acknowledging it, then that too becomes your choice—and choice is what a healthy sex life is all about.

Out of Control

Before we go any further, I think we ought to take a moment to discuss a pattern of behavior that may mask itself as a form of sexual free expression, but is in fact sexual addiction. There's a vast difference between an adult woman who, as a result of introspection and informed choice, decides that she likes sex and is going to pursue it without apology on her own terms, and a woman who uses promiscuity to fill a void in her life in an attempt to make up for a lack of proper role models, emotional support, and discipline that she should have had when she was growing up.

Women—especially young women and teenage girls—who rush blindly into sexual encounter after sexual encounter do so out of low self-esteem, no matter how vehemently they deny it. Too often, they put themselves into positions that expose them to unsafe sex, unwanted pregnancies, alcohol or drug dependency, physical and psychological abuse, or even worse. You can't turn on the television these days without seeing a talk show about girls as young as nine and ten who are sexually active and proud of it. You'll hear these girls bragging that they had sex with over a hundred men before they were sixteen, or took on the whole football team in one night, as if these were actually accomplishments devoutly to be wished.

Sure, sex makes us feel good; so does eating chocolate. But you wouldn't feed a youngster nothing but candy just because that's what he or she wants, any more than you'd let a five-year-old drive a car on the freeway. There's no denying that sex is out there, and teenagers are going to get into it. And it well may be that some are ready for it sooner than others. But sex isn't just a right, it's also a responsibility, and too often parents lose sight of that. Many parents are afraid that disciplining children and teaching them to wait until they can make mature choices regarding sex will make their children love them less, but in reality, when you give a child a sense of honor, self-respect, and good judgment, that child will love you more.

If you're trapped in a cycle in which your craving for physical affection has become an overpowering, driving force in your life, or you find yourself sleeping with so many different guys you can't remember their names, chances are it's not coming from a woman who is expressing sexual empowerment, but rather, one who is presenting symptoms of a deeply wounded psyche and a twisted self-image. If your sex life is characterized by the type of self-destructive behavior I've just described, it may be time to reevaluate what's important to you. You should be in control of your sex life; your sex life should not be in control of you.

Sex is an act that, though profound and affecting, is part of love, not a substitute for it. Whether it's you who have the problem, or a child whom you can't get through to, don't give up on yourself or the child. In either case, there's no shame in seeking help. If you want to make a change, it's possible, no matter how hopeless the circumstances may seem. With time, insight, and understanding, even some of the hardest cases can get turned around.

Seduction How-Tos

Question: *How difficult is it to seduce the average man?*
Answer: *Not very.*

Truth is, once a man's aroused, it doesn't usually take too much effort get him to act on his feelings. Consequently, women don't really need a complicated guide to seducing the male animal, per se. For most, just letting things happen naturally can be enough.

The thing to remember is that the key to human seduction lies within our five senses. By exploring them and learning what is most pleasing and stimulating, it's fairly simple to get most men right where we want them—in bed, or in the shower, or on the kitchen table . . .

Sight

Men are very visually oriented. They love to look. Daring decolletage and a skirt slit up to there can be very big turn-ons. Whether you decide to go the route of putting it all up front, leaving little to the imagination, or take the "flash and a hint of things to come" approach would depend of course on the man you're dating and the scenario of the seduction. If you're planning a special evening, by all means dress the part, but make sure that you're comfortable in whatever you choose to wear. Should you feel silly or ill-at-ease in an outfit, your discomfort may intrude on your pleasure and detract from the moment.

Smell

Sorry, ladies, but according to research, perfume is not the way to a man's heart—or his libido. Want to know one of the sexiest smells on the planet where men are concerned? The aroma of cinnamon, especially when it's being cooked in something yummy, is reported to be a major stimulant. Go figure! So, if you're in the mood to make whoopee, walking him by a bakery and buying some hot cinnamon buns may just help do the trick.

If you do like to include perfume as part of your seduction repertoire, use a light touch, because—assuming you've got decent hygiene habits—most men adore the natural scent of a woman.

Touch

Since part of the traditional roles we've inherited sets up men as providers and women as receivers, many guys are more geared toward touching us than accepting being touched by us, and there's no question that men derive pleasure from exploring the female body with their hands, tongues, and genitals. But men's bodies, like our own, have a myriad of hot spots that can be stimulated by touch. Giving your lover an all-over massage — with or without sexual implications — can clue you in to where his particular erogenous zones lie. This can also help him appreciate his own body more, by uncovering pleasure points he may have been unaware of previously.

Two other tools for you to consider are texture and touch. Rubbing something silky against his most sensitive flesh can lead to the most exquisite sensations; likewise a skillfully applied ice cube or warmed body oil.

Hearing

While music doth have charms to soothe, and it can certainly help put your man in the mood, the sound that is really music to most men's ears is a woman expressing her pleasure. The noises we make while in the throes of lovemaking — our words, sighs, moans — only serve to toss fuel onto his fire. Tell him what you like. Tell him that he pleases you. And once you're committed to it, don't be afraid to get lost in the moment.

Taste

Food can be very sexy, and there definitely are many ways in which it can be included in your sensual feasts; however, should you choose to do so, it's still a safe bet that *you* may wind up as the main course. Since our sense of taste is dependent on our sense of smell, many of the same rules apply for both, so go easy on the soaps, scents, and what-have-you. Your lover wants to taste you, not a mouthful of chemicals.

Seduction Dos . . .

Have safe sex at all times!

Condoms aren't sexy? Think of the alternative. Until further notice, we live in the age of latex. Instead of being vexed by it, we must learn to eroticize it as best we can and incorporate it into our lovemaking practices.

Though some men complain that condoms "desensitize" the sex act, if you can turn putting the condom on him into a sensual, shared ritual, some couples report that the experience can be transformed from onerous to enjoyable. One other possible added benefit to the very desensitization that men complain about is that there is some evidence to suggest that condoms may help men who are quick on the trigger last longer. Give a little, get a little . . .

When you begin dating a man, if you intend to have sexual relations with him, both of you need to be tested for HIV. If he tells you he's already been tested, don't just take his word for it—if he cares about you, he'll take the test again. If he won't, you should be asking yourself why.

The accepted "waiting term" for monogamous couples who prefer to engage in "condomless sex" is six months from the date of your first HIV test. If you both test negative again at that point, some people do choose to move on to other methods of contraception; however, unless you can guarantee the fidelity of your partner 100 percent, do you want to take the risk? Sure, it would be awful to find out that your man had cheated on you, but think of how much worse you'd feel if he brought home something deadly and passed it along to you.

Be Creative

Sex doesn't have to be done the same way all the time. Experiment! There's nothing wrong with testing out other locales besides the bedroom for your lovemaking exploits, or grabbing a quickie now and then. Role-playing games, food, toys, and erotic fantasies can all be tossed into the mix as you go along. Don't be afraid to try something new. You may not like it, but then again, you just might!

Keep your sense of humor.

When we make love to a new man, especially for the first time, any number of minor glitches may crop up in the course of those magic moments. From falling out of bed, to waking up face-to-face with your lover's bulldog, to "tummy-farts," to broken bedsprings, things can and do just sort of go wrong. Sex is not brain surgery, so a minor slipup, no matter how embarrassing at the time, is really no big deal. Instead of letting these minor monkey wrenches ruin your mood, try to maintain a positive outlook and learn to laugh at these situations. They are really not the end of the world.

Communicate, communicate, communicate!

We've all got our own personal idiosyncrasies where sex is concerned. You have to let your partner know what you like *and* what you don't like. As I've said before, men *do* want to please you, but they're not mind readers. While it isn't always necessary to give him a verbal play-by-play, you can still find ways to express your pleasure to him.

... And Don'ts

Don't force it.

If you're not ready to have sex yet, don't. It will only leave you resenting your partner and disappointed with yourself. If you've had sex with a new lover and you're having second thoughts, try not to dwell on negativity. Unless he gave a "sex-or-else" ultimatum, there's no point in blaming either him or yourself, and it's perfectly all right to take a step back at this point. But do explain your feelings to your lover. Most men take anything related to sex very personally, so if he's someone you care about keeping in your life, do your best to assure him that he hasn't done anything wrong.

Don't fake it.

Faking orgasms is *verboten*. Pretending pleasure only cheats both of you. He'll just keep doing whatever it is he's been doing under the mistaken impression that you actually like it, so you're not going to be satisfied, and finding out that you've been faking will do infinitely more damage to his ego than occasionally not achieving climax. Orgasms are wonderful, but there's a whole lot more to sex than just hitting the high notes.

Don't fixate on it.

Having sex with a man is no guarantee that your relationship is going to move to a more meaningful level. Don't spend a lot of time agonizing, analyzing, or reading things into his behavior. Sex is an integral part of a healthy relationship, but it's only a part. Yet some women have a tendency to load it down with excessive emotional baggage. Let things take their course and unfold naturally, and keep your eye on the bigger picture.

Don't be judgmental about it.

If you let your first time together make or break a love affair, you may be setting yourself up for a fall. You can't manufacture attraction, but sometimes good sex between new partners takes practice. Of course, there are going to be instances when we finally get down to doing the deed and the dude's a dud. That's a fact of life. Even people who have a strong physical attraction to one another may be totally incompatible between the sheets. If this happens, you can sometimes work it out, but it will take an open mind, mutual consideration, and a lot of effort from both parties concerned. In some cases, however, no matter what you try, it just doesn't change. At that point, if you've both given it your best shot, it may be time to call it a day. (Unless you're willing to

engage in a sex-free or nonexclusive arrangement,
which, practically speaking, most of us aren't.)

Troubleshooting

Performance anxiety (his)

We've all heard it more times than we can remember:
men have fragile egos. There's a reason for this—it's
true. A new man wants to be the best lover you've ever
had, or at least think he is. A word to the wise: leave the
skeletons from your romantic past in the closet. If your
last partner had tremendous stamina, terrific technique,
and a ten-inch . . . well, your current lover doesn't need to
know about it.

And as mentioned above, if sex isn't perfect the first
time, don't put too much weight on it. Factors such as
anxiety, eagerness, and alcohol can all have a negative
impact on a man's performance. Be kind. Cut him some
slack, and whatever you do, don't tease him.

Performance anxiety (hers)

Though men may have a worse reputation on this
count, women, too, want to be all that they can be in bed,
and often react by being overly eager to please. They are
constantly worrying that they aren't skilled enough, that
they're not loud enough or they're too loud, that they
don't have enough experience or they've got too much,
that they look awful with their clothes off or that they
can't live up to the image of his last girlfriend or to the
images of the women in magazines such as *Playboy*. Does
any of this sound like you?

If so, then you've got to cut *yourself* some slack. Tell
yourself he's with you because he wants to be with you.
He doesn't expect you to look like a centerfold or have an
advanced degree in oral sex, so why should you? Again,

if you feel your appearance or technique could stand improvement, by all means, do what you have to do — but do it for yourself, not because you hope it will make him like you more.

And while it's perfectly acceptable to explore new territory with your lover, you are *not* obligated to engage in any activity that makes you uncomfortable. Though you might want to take time to rethink what it is about certain acts that disturbs you. Often, we block the avenues to pleasure after one bad experience, and turn a minor snafu into a major taboo. If this is the case for you, try to wipe the slate clean and look at things with a fresh perspective. You may find that by giving such things a second shot, they aren't so bad, and you might actually enjoy them.

PART FOUR

Future Plans

CHAPTER ELEVEN

Come Live with Me and Be My Love

BACK IN THE DARK AGES, long before the emergence of yuppies, buppies, dinks (double income, no kids), working women, no-fault divorce, and the Internet, it was the accepted rule of thumb in most so-called civilized cultures that men and women must never live together as a couple prior to getting hitched—officially.

If we fast-forward to the end of the twentieth century, there's pretty solid evidence that it's better not to rush into getting married. Some statistics say that couples who live together prior to marriage have a greater divorce rate than couples who don't; other statistics confirm just the opposite. The truth is, good numbers crunchers can take any set of data and present the facts in such a way as to prove whatever point they're trying to make. But there is one basic reality that can't be disputed. People are living a lot longer than ever before. So, if you're going into a marriage with the intention of making a lifetime commitment to someone, it's a good idea to look very closely before you leap. Where romance is concerned, there's no sin in seeing what you're getting yourself into, especially when you think it might be leading to something as important as marriage. You wouldn't buy a car without test-driving it, would you? Remember, breaking up may be hard to do, but divorce is ten times uglier.

Living with someone can offer you valuable insights you might never gain from just going out with that person, or even spending a few nights a week in each other's company. When we're dating, we're on good behavior. When you live with someone, the real you comes out. It's inevitable. That real person is the one your mate is going to have to be comfortable around for the long haul, and vice versa. And some people, regardless of how much they love and respect each other, just don't have what it takes to make it as a successful couple.

There are aspects to everyone's behavior—no matter how wonderful we may be—that someone else may not be able to cope with. Not that we're purposely hiding our shortcomings—or at least, the things that other people might perceive as shortcomings—it's just that some issues never come up until after people have spent considerable time together. Until you're in a situation that doesn't afford you the luxury of an immediate escape hatch, you won't be able to judge what your partner is truly made of.

The majority of couples experience the most difficult part of living together right at the very beginning. It's a cinch that the woman is going to find herself flopping butt-first into the toilet in the middle of the night because *he* forgot to put the seat down. The odds are four to one that the man is going to have to suffer infinite torment when *she* refuses to fork over the remote. You'll get over this part.

And in the long run, it's not the little issues that will decide if you're meant to be together. If you're ready to move in with each other, it's probably a good bet that you've got chemistry going, but be prepared for the inevitable mutations that will take place—for better or worse—when you go from being on your own to being in someone's near-constant company. Everything—from your sex life to your bills and your daily schedule—is bound to change. When you move in with your lover, small idiosyncrasies can take on whole new meanings; minor bad habits can prove to have major implications. There are a few key factors that you will need to examine very closely to see if the match you've made has staying power. Here are three of the most important to consider:

1. Sharing the chores.

When you become part of a couple, things that you have traditionally done for yourself are suddenly shared responsibility. From paying the bills and taking out the trash, to who walks the dog and which way you hang the toilet paper, your everyday decisions are no longer up to you alone.

What you should bear in mind is that you ought to set up house rules from the get-go. Many people make the mistake of assuming that living with a lover isn't like living with a roommate, because you care for one another so much. But it's as a direct result of having this emotional attachment that we run into the danger of having our feelings hurt.

Think about it: Say you've got a roommate who habitually leaves dirty laundry and empty yogurt containers in the living room. You ask him to clean up his act, and for a while he does; then he reverts to his old behavior. You ask him again, and again he complies, then it's back to the same old same old. At that point you write him off as a childish jerk, a nuisance. But when a lover behaves in a way that is displeasing to us, especially if he continues to do it over a period of time, we take it personally. *He knows how much that bothers me*, we tell ourselves, *and he does it anyway. If he cared about me, he wouldn't treat me this way*.

We tend to believe that because a man cares for us, he will know what we need and what upsets us — but sometimes this assumption couldn't be further from the truth. As much as we'd like them to be able to, our lovers can't always read our minds. If you're clear from the beginning about what flies and what doesn't, he should be able to get with the program. However, if you let a man know your boundaries, and he continually oversteps them, that's a whole different kettle of fish.

Says Anna: "My boyfriend Preston was raised in a family where men didn't lift a finger, but I had no clue until we'd been living together for about a week how much he expected me to take care of around the house. I'd come home from a long day at the office and found the ashtrays overflowing, which really bugged me because *I* don't smoke; the trash hadn't been taken out; the breakfast dishes were still in the sink; and there was Preston, sitting on the couch reading the paper. What really got my goat was that, being a teacher, Preston had the week off for spring break. He'd been fast asleep when I got up to go to work, and from the looks of the junk food debris, he'd spent the entire day on the sofa.

"Now, I don't begrudge anyone taking time to just chill out, but this was *way* beyond the pale. I was furious, but instead of saying anything, I just went and got out of my work clothes, put on some sweats, and started to clean up. I'd been at it for about fifteen minutes when he looked up from the sports page and said innocently, 'What's for dinner, honey?' On top of everything else, he wanted me to cook, too!

"I just lost it. I ran into the bedroom, threw myself down on the bed, and cried. I was tremendously hurt by Preston's inconsiderate behavior. It was like someone had snuck in and replaced my wonderful boyfriend with a troglodyte. Then it struck me that I'd already given up my apartment and I was stuck. The only alternative I could think of was slinking home with my tail between my legs and moving back in with my parents.

"About two minutes later, Preston came in and asked me what was wrong. He was genuinely flabbergasted when I told him that I didn't appreciate being treated like his maid or his cook. I let him know how unfair I thought it was that I'd been at work all day and he hadn't bothered to lift his ass off the couch, except to get himself a beer. I admitted to him that I'd been harboring a secret hope that since he knew I was working late and he had the day off that maybe he'd make us a nice, romantic meal and have it on the table waiting when I got home — but not only was there no dinner, there was a huge mess to contend with.

"I told him that as far as I was concerned, it just wasn't fair. And, to my amazement, Preston agreed with me. He apologized and then went on to tell me that his mom did everything for his dad and his brothers. She'd even get angry if they tried to help, so none of the men ever got into the habit."

Frankly, Anna found Preston's explanation, no matter how sincere he seemed, a little hard to believe. They'd been dating for almost a year before they moved in together, and every time she'd been to his apartment it had been, if not spotless, at least orderly. In fact, truth be told, he was probably a better housekeeper than she was. She says, "His total abdication of responsibility knocked me for a loop. Here he'd been on his own and taking care of himself for years, then once he moves in with me, he suddenly becomes Lord of the Manor. What was that about?"

What it was about was exactly what Preston had told her. In the family dynamic in which Preston had grown up, the female role model — his mother — not only executed all the chores, she insisted on it. It was fairly common for women of that era to pride themselves on their housekeeping skills to the point where they would brook no interference from the male members of the household. Preston simply reverted to kind when faced with a situation he equated with "home."

The reason that Preston had been taken aback by Anna's outburst was that until that very moment, he didn't realize he was doing anything wrong. Once Anna let him know that she needed him to do more, it gave him permission to change his habits, and he was more than willing to try. "He asked me what he could do to make things better," she recalls. "I told him he was going to have to pitch in, or I wasn't going to be able to continue the relationship. We sat down and made a specific list of who does what and by when."

If Preston and Anna had set up house rules *before* they moved in together, they probably could have avoided a lot of the grief. You need to establish who is responsible for what chores and then do your best to live up to that bargain. Of course, not everyone needs a specific chart of chores. Some couples fall into a routine that works quite naturally. And we all slip up now and again. There will be evenings when the dishes won't get done or the trash will go out the following morning. The important thing is that each of you let the other know what you expect and honor one another's wishes as best you can, and this will mean compromise. Try to give your partner a break until he gets used to the new schedule. Someone like Preston, who was used to having everything done for him, can't change overnight, no matter how willing he is to mend his ways.

"To his credit," Anna says, "from that point on, he made a real effort, but I always had to ask him for help around the house. It took me awhile to get over my own anger at always having to remind him to take out the trash or do the dishes or empty the ashtrays. Who wants to have to be a policeman? Part of me still believed that if he loved me, he ought to do those things automatically."

The trick for Anna was not to take Preston's sins of omission (omitting to empty the ashtray, omitting to pick up his socks, etc.) personally, and not to become bitter or hostile when she asked him to do something that in her mind he should already have done. As Anna admitted, Preston's behavior was causing her to experience a lot of anger and frustration. This period of adjustment would have to be a learning process for both of them. He would literally need to clean up his act, and she, rather than lashing out, would have to find constructive ways to help him make the change.

"I had to keep fighting off my instinctive urge to nag him, because that only made him resentful and his habits would get even worse. Eventually, he came around—or we both did, really, but it was definitely an uphill battle, and there were times when I didn't think we were going to make it."

2. Finances

Nothing can break up a happy couple faster than having different attitudes about money. Aesop had a fable for this one—"The Ant and the Grasshopper." During the summer and fall, the sensible ant planned for the winter by gathering food and storing it for the days ahead. The grasshopper, on the other hand, lived only for the moment, eating, playing, and generally having a good time, without a thought to the future. So when the snow began to fall, the ant was prepared, and the grasshopper was . . . screwed.

If you are the ant and your mate is the grasshopper— or the other way around—unless you are able to work out a financial plan both of you can live with and stick to, you may be headed for disaster.

"My ex-boyfriend, Ron," says Kate, a twenty-seven-year-old illustrator of children's books, "was the instant gratification kid. Whatever he wanted, he bought, and not just for himself. Looking back at it, his generosity was one of the things that really attracted me to him. He was a great tipper. He'd send roses to my office for no reason. He'd book a spur-of-the-moment romantic weekend for us in Jamaica, but he was also an equipment freak. He had to have every new computer gizmo that came on the market. His stereo entertainment center had to be big-screen, digitally mastered, state of the art, the best that money could buy.

"The problem was that he didn't have the money to pay for any of these things. He earned a decent living, but it wasn't enough to cover his expenses. His credit card balances were astronomical. Of course, I never knew how bad he was until we started living together and the bills began pouring in.

"Ron had gone to the paycheck-to-paycheck school of personal finance. I, on the other hand, hate to owe money to anyone. My school loans are paid off. I always make sure my rent is in by the first of the month. I never carry outstanding balances on my credit cards, unless I've made a really big purchase, and even then I'll make up a payment schedule for myself and stick to it. Ron's 'I'll pay it when I get to it' attitude made me crazy.

"Since the lease was in both of our names, it got to the point where I was the one always forking out money for the rent, the gas and electric, and the phone. He always paid me back . . . eventually, but I really began to resent him for putting me in that position. I'd try to explain to him why his behavior bugged me, but it never seemed to sink in.

"On a lot of levels, Ron is a great guy, but I just couldn't take it after a while. We split up, and I have to confess, I'm kind of relieved. If I was losing sleep when we were just living together, imagine how it would have been if we'd actually gotten married."

Along with figuring out the who-does-what of the chores, when you move in with a man you should make provisions regarding not only when bills are paid, but who pays for what. This is not to say that every arrangement needs to be fifty-fifty. If you're earning a lot more than he is salary-wise, but he puts a lot more effort into running the household, it's okay if he contributes more time and you contribute more money. But it's up to *both* of you to decide what is fair.

And don't let yourself fall into the trap of holding each other accountable for every penny that each of you spends. You can let him pay for your dry cleaning from time to time, and you can pick up the cost of the gourmet coffee he can't live without that you never touch. Work with ballpark figures and give each other leeway; after all, you're supposed to be lovers, not business partners.

3. Illness

There's a reason for that "in sickness and in health" proviso that's a part of most wedding services, since there is no greater test of a man's character than how he reacts the first time *you* get sick. As women, we are used to being caregivers. It goes with the territory. Even those who aren't Florence Nightingale generally have at least a working knowledge of which end of the thermometer goes where and the merits of chicken soup (whether homemade or from a can).

Men, however, can be totally clueless when it comes to the gentle arts of healing. As recounted by Heather, her perfect man became the invisible man when confronted with illness. "Johnny and I had just gotten the apartment," she recalls. "The ink wasn't even dry on the lease. The furniture hadn't been delivered yet, and we were using some big futon pillows instead of a bed.

"We'd been there less than a week, when one morning I woke up with a really high fever, over 103 degrees. My head was pounding and my body felt like it had been beaten with two-by-fours. I was nauseous and dizzy. Every time I tried to stand up, I had to sit back down again because my feet kept sinking into the floor, which seemed at the time to be made of some rubberlike substance. At one point, my cat came up and rubbed against me, which wasn't so unusual since he always knew when I wasn't feeling well. The problem was that my cat had been dead for over ten years. I was really happy to see him, but at the same time, I knew I was hallucinating.

"And where was Johnny during all of this? you may ask. He made himself very scarce, and I mean *very*," Heather reports. "He not only didn't bring me a cup of tea, he didn't even offer to make me one. I have never been that sick in my life — before or since — and he just disappeared. I was so weak and so frustrated, I was in tears.

"There were workmen scheduled to come to replace the windows, and he left me to deal with them. I have no idea what I said to them; I was probably incoherent. Thank God they offered to come back the following week.

"Now, I don't want you to get the idea that Johnny was some kind of monster. In almost every other aspect of the relationship, he was loving, caring, giving, and fair. It was just that when it came to my being sick, it was like his psyche had a hole in it. It made me wonder whether if we were ever in a traffic accident he would leave me by the side of the road to bleed to death."

When Heather recovered from her illness, she sat Johnny down and told him point-blank that she thought he'd behaved abominably. She demanded to know why someone who was supposed to care for her had jumped ship at the first sign of trouble. His justification to her was that when *he* was sick, the last thing he wanted was someone hovering around, doing things for him, and the worse his illness, the less attention he could endure. When he wasn't feeling well, he developed what he called "wounded bear syndrome" — he just wanted to crawl into his cave and lick his wounds in peace.

But this explanation was only the tip of a much larger iceberg. Johnny had been brought up in a home where emotions were not displayed openly. They didn't hug. They didn't say "I love you." They didn't complain when they were ill. They didn't celebrate a job well done. Instead, they were taught that self-denial and self-sufficiency were the highest virtues one could strive for. When the children were growing up, if they got sick, their mother would take care of their basic physical needs, but she'd never cater to their emotional needs, because she did not recognize that as a part of wellness. It was this viewpoint that carried over into Johnny's adult life, and it colored his behavior toward his loved ones in almost everything he did.

"I never really understood how Johnny wound up that way until I visited their home," Heather says. "He came from a very small town, a farming community. He was the first in his family to have a successful career, something he'd achieved all on his own. I could tell by his parents' faces how proud they were of him, how much they loved him. They were fit to bust, but they never said a word. And I could see, being on the outside of it, that he had no idea how important he was to them. It was really sad, but it explained an awful lot.

"Johnny never got over his 'affection deficit,' " Heather says sadly. "A lot of the time, I felt like, emotionally, I was dying of thirst. It got to the point where he would do me the courtesy of making me tea when I wasn't feeling well, or he'd hug me if I asked him to, but he never understood why it was important to me."

If a man is incapable of giving care to you when you're sick, there's a good chance that something else is going on. Coping may just be a matter of you shifting your expectations, or helping him to hone his nursing skills, but if a man is not forthcoming in this area it may well be a warning sign of other, more serious limits to his emotional scope.

Moving in with someone—even someone you love dearly—is rarely perfect from day one, but there's no need to panic when the wrapper comes off and what's in the package isn't exactly what you expected. Before you jump to hasty conclusions, remember to factor in some breathing room. Give yourself and your lover time to adjust, mark territory, and set limits. Problems can be worked out. Bumps in the road can be smoothed over. That's what the whole process is all about. Compromise is not a dirty word, as long as *both* of you are willing to bend.

Whether you consider living together a test flight before marriage or the main event, it's a venture that has to be beneficial to both parties who enter into it. After you've been together for a reasonable period, try to "step outside" of the situation and give it a good once-over to sort out the wheat from the chaff. Getting a sense of the balance—the give and take—of things is crucial to the health, well-being, and potential long-term success of any union. Once you've become a one-domicile couple, keep a close watch on how the dynamics of your relationship develop.

Do you feel like you're always having to play the cop or the mommy? Do your needs fall by the wayside so that his can be served first? At the first sign of trouble does he "suddenly remember he needs to be somewhere" — anywhere but where the problem is? Are you just using him as a way station until the "real thing" comes along, or are you hopping on the first bus that comes along because you're afraid you won't get another chance? None of these are good signs. Sure, you've got to follow your heart, but don't ignore your head. If any of these red flags are the hallmarks of your relationship, you should ask yourself if it's one you should be in. And if it isn't, be honest with yourself and move on. (Yes, that's easier said than done.)

Living together is a wonderful life experiment, no matter how things work themselves out in the end. Chances are, if you're meant to be together, then you will be. If you're not, try to see the lessons that are being sent your way, and learn from both the good and the bad. If you can, you'll become a bigger person for it, with a better understanding of what you're looking for the next time. And don't worry about that bus. It might be delayed, but another one almost always comes along.

CHAPTER TWELVE

Is "I Do" for You?

FROM THE TIME WE'RE very small children, almost even before we develop conscious thought, we are bombarded by images that depict the traditional family unit as the essence of human comfort and happiness. We all have our roles to play: Men are husbands, women are wives, boys are sons, girls are daughters, and so the pattern goes and goes and that's what makes the world spin 'round. Or does it?

What happens if you . . . deviate? What becomes of those of us who never get married, or, if such a thing is to be believed, don't even want to? What happens is very much the same as what happened to the heroine in a little story I call "Goldilocks and Three the Bears." (No, that's not a misprint.)

• • •

Once upon a time there was a beautiful blonde girl named Goldilocks who lived with her mother and father in a farmhouse on the edge of a vast forest. Goldilocks was a bright child, obedient and thoughtful, who strove always to follow her parents' wishes and mold her hopes to suit their wisdom.

"Goldilocks, light of my life," her mother said one night as she gave her daughter's golden curls a thousand strokes with a boar-bristle brush, "someday soon you will grow up to be a woman."

"Yes, Mama," said Goldilocks.

"And when you've grown up and become a woman, you will meet many handsome young men," her mother continued.

"Yes, Mama," said Goldilocks.

"And of all these young men you meet, some will try to steal your heart away."

"Really, Mama?" asked Goldilocks.

"Certainly, my dear. But of these many young men, only one will win your heart."

"Yes, Mama," said Goldilocks.

"And when the time comes, should your father and I give our consent, you will marry this man and leave our house."

"Must I go?" Goldilocks asked, growing concerned.

"Of course, my darling. Just as I left the house of my father and mother, and my mother left the house of her parents before that. This is a woman's lot in life. You must trust our judgment, darling. We know what's best for your welfare."

"Yes, Mama," said Goldilocks, not totally convinced. With that, Goldilocks's mother put down the brush and kissed her beloved daughter on the brow. Goldilocks fell into a fitful slumber. Her mother stood at the foot of her bed, watching the sleeping child. The candle guttered and spat. A momentary shadow of regret passed across the mother's face and just as quickly disappeared. "A woman's lot," she whispered to no one but herself. Then she blew out the candle and drew the door closed behind her.

That night, Goldilocks had a strange and disturbing dream. She dreamt that she was a grown woman, the wife of a handsome man who had wooed and won her heart.

They had two small, fair-haired toddlers, a boy and a girl, and they lived on a beautiful estate, where a vast lawn swept down a lazy hill, past apple orchards, a formal garden, and a thicket of willow trees, to a placid pond on the surface of which languidly floated a dozen white swans.

As Goldilocks gazed out across the lawn from the window of her majestic home, her husband sat reading a thick volume of history by a blazing fire while the children played contentedly at her feet. But then, a dark cloud came rolling from the far horizon across the landscape of her dream, and another and another, until the sky was fully black. "Husband," she called, "I am afraid." But her lord and master did not lift his eyes from his book. "Children," she said, "come away from the window, for a storm is coming and I want to keep you safe." But the children paid her no heed. In fact, it was as if they did not hear her at all.

"Husband," she called, her voice growing shrill with alarm, "husband, help me with the children, for they will not listen to me." Her husband made no move, nor showed any sign of having heard her. Now, nearly in a panic, Goldilocks bent down to pull the children away from the window, but as she reached out to them, her hands, as if made of mist, passed right through them. And then, to her horror, she realized that though this was her life, she had no voice in it, and no more substance than a ghost.

She woke with a start, and cast her eyes about the shadowy bedroom. Outside her window, the silver moon shone down, his face smiling with some knowledge she did not understand but found somehow comforting all the same. In time, she fell back asleep.

The next morning, after her chores were done, Goldilocks was feeling a bit restless. "Papa," she asked, "may I go for a walk in the forest?"

"Well," said her father, "all right, but don't be gone too long. Your mother and I have a surprise for you. It should be here just before dinnertime."

"Thank you, Papa," said Goldilocks, and with that, off she went, tripping merrily through the summer woods. She had not gone more than a hundred yards when across her path flitted the most beautiful butterfly she had ever seen. Its wings were fully as large as the double handspan of the village blacksmith and, like the smithy's hands, black as coal at the tips, but dotted all along its wings were cascading arcs of feathery violet and iridescent green so astounding that Goldilocks's eyes filled with wonder.

Without another thought, Goldilocks followed the dazzling butterfly as it wound its way deeper and deeper into the forest. She had been chasing it for nearly all the morning, when suddenly, without warning, it flew straight up over the tops of the trees and out of her sight. Her reverie broken, Goldilocks realized that not only had she disobeyed her father by staying away for so long, but she was tired and hungry and hadn't the faintest clue where in the wide world she was. Thoroughly disgusted with herself, she sat down on a log to try to collect her thoughts and figure out a way to get home, but hungry as she was, it was hard to concentrate on her dilemma.

I haven't eaten in so long, I'm beginning to imagine things, she told herself when several minutes later she thought she'd caught a whiff of food — porridge, to be specific — wafting over the nearby knoll. A second later, when the breeze blew from that same direction, she smelled it again and off she went to investigate.

As Goldilocks reached the crest of the hill, a charming cabin came into view. *I wonder who lives there?* she thought. Goldilocks could see smoke rising lazily from the chimney, and the smell of porridge grew stronger.

Her mouth began to water. *Maybe I'll just go a little closer and have a look. . . .* When she got within twenty paces of the cabin, she saw a mailbox on the side of which was printed in large block letters:

THREE
THE BEARS

Now, Goldilocks was a fairly sensible girl and knew that it was perhaps not a good idea to tangle with bears, especially at breakfast time (or was it brunch time by now?), but she couldn't help but notice that the cabin was strangely quiet and devoid of the bearlike commotion one would normally associate with grizzlies chowing down. When Goldilocks tiptoed closer and peered in the cabin window, her suspicions were confirmed. There was not a bear anywhere in sight.

However, sitting on the dining table were three tempting bowls of luscious-looking porridge and a plate of ripe, wild strawberries. *I really shouldn't,* she told herself even as she was sneaking across the threshold, creeping up to the table and stealthily taking a spoon in her hand, *but I'm so hungry . . . .*

Goldilocks dipped her spoon into the first bowl of porridge and plunged the steaming mouthful between her lips. "Yikes!" she screamed, then yanked a pitcher of ice water from the table and took a hearty gulp. You guessed it. The porridge was too darn hot.

Into the second bowl went the spoon. This time, Goldilocks brought it carefully to her lips, taking just the tiniest speck to try. "Yuk!" she gagged, spitting out the offending morsel into a napkin. It was stone cold.

Finally, when she was at the point of near total disgust, her hunger got the better of her and she decided to give the last bowl a try. Gingerly, she scooped up a scant spoonful of the stuff and popped it quickly into her mouth before she could change her mind. Much to her relief, it was perfect. Goldilocks ate the rest of the contents of the bowl, then proceeded to polish off the strawberries. All at once, she became very tired.

As luck would have it, Goldilocks spied three beds lined up in a row across the floor of the great open room. Now, maybe she wasn't thinking too clearly at that point, since the bears could have come back at any moment, but Goldilocks decided that what she really needed was a nap. So she walked over to the first bed and was about to climb in when she realized that it was as hard as a rock. Next she tried the middle bed, but it was so soft it nearly swallowed her up. The third bed was the charm, and within seconds of her head touching its downy pillow, Goldilocks was fast asleep.

When she awoke sometime later, the day was on the wane. The rays of the afternoon sun slanted long and red. Goldilocks sat up with a jolt. She was not alone. Looking up, Goldilocks was temporarily blinded by the glare, but she could just make out the silhouettes of three shaggy forms sitting at the table. She was about to let out a scream, when she heard a very human voice say, "Oh, you're up!"

Goldilocks blinked hard against the light and realized that it wasn't three bears sitting at the table—it was three men. "I don't understand, the sign on the letterbox said . . ."

"People make that mistake all the time," another one said. "We're not bears, it's just the family name; three's our address."

"Oh," said Goldilocks.

"Yes," the third continued, "that's right. We're just three bachelor brothers living in the woods . . ."

"Licking our wounds," the first muttered sarcastically.

"Oh, don't mind him, little lady," the second one threw in. "He's just bitter because his wife left him. We call him 'Rebound,' and you can too if you'd like."

"Well, I . . ." she started to say, but she was cut off.

"That's right, rub it in," Rebound grumbled to the first brother. "At least I gave it a shot—I'm not a wussy Mama's Bear who never left home, like you!"

"Guys, guys, cut it out," admonished the third brother. "Not in front of company."

"And what do they call *you?*" Goldilocks asked this brother—the one with the voice of reason.

"Ox . . . as in 'Un-orth-o-*dox*,'" he said, pronouncing each syllable separately and putting an emphasis on the last.

"Why Unorthodox?" asked Goldilocks.

"Always a best man, never a groom," Rebound chimed in. "Though he got real close a couple of times."

"I'm not surprised," said Goldilocks, before she could stop herself, for Ox was quite a handsome fellow.

"Thank you," said Ox, turning on a smile that could light a dark cave at midnight. "Speaking of surprises, to what do we owe the pleasure of this visit?"

Goldilocks sheepishly explained how she'd wandered away from her home and had been unable to find her way back. "My parents must be frantic by now," she said.

"What does your house look like?" Mama's Bear asked.

Goldilocks described the farmhouse and the yard and her parents to the brothers Bear.

"Do you have a black rooster that walks with a limp?" Ox inquired.

"How did you know?" cried Goldilocks.

"Picket fence that's got three slats missing from the east corner? And a weathervane shaped like a running boar?"

"Yes!" she answered with delight.

"I know where that is," Ox said. "I'll walk you home."

"You'd better hurry up, bucko, it'll be dark soon," Rebound remarked pessimistically.

"Here," said Mama's Bear, handing Goldilocks a little container tied up with string. "Have some porridge for later. It reheats very nicely."

"Thank you," said Goldilocks. "You've all been so kind."

So Ox and Goldilocks set off through the forest. To pass the time, Ox told her stories, recited a few poems, and even sang her a few songs he was thinking of submitting to the king's minstrel. "They're really not very good," he said. But Goldilocks thought they were the finest and most inspiring things she'd ever heard.

"Ox," she asked, not really sure why she was asking, "do you think you'll ever get married?"

"Probably not," he answered after a moment's thought. "I'm just too eccentric."

"But don't you want to fall in love?" Goldilocks pressed.

"One thing has nothing to do with the other," Ox told her. "Maybe when you're older you'll see that. Or maybe you never will, because it won't be true for you." They stopped walking then and looked deep into one another's eyes.

"Goldilocks!" her father's voice suddenly boomed from across the meadow. "Goldilocks, where have you been? Your mother and I have been worried sick," he panted, having run the hundred feet that separated them.

"I'm so sorry, Father," she began, "but I got lost, and this gentleman . . ." She turned to introduce Ox, but he was gone.

"Did he harm you, child?" her father asked, his voice filled with an unsettlingly suspicious tone that she did not recognize.

"No, Father!" she replied earnestly. "He was kind enough to bring me home. That's all."

"Nothing more?"

"Nothing. I swear," she answered.

"Then all is well," he said. "Come, daughter, I have someone for you to meet. He has been waiting the better part of the afternoon and we have tried his patience long enough. Hurry along, girl."

When they got to the house, Goldilocks's mother flew out the front door and hugged her child. "Thank God you're safe," she sighed. Then she brushed the stray strands of hair from her daughter's face and dabbed her face with a handkerchief. "Now come inside and meet our honored guest."

It so happened that the honored guest was the son of a wealthy landowner of her parents' acquaintance who hailed from the next county over. He was a fairly attractive lad, in a beefy way — a few years older than Goldilocks; a solid, steady type whose life was bound to the earth and the seasons, the sowing and the harvest. He seemed an honest lad, but after listening to him speak for only a moment, it was clear to Goldilocks that he was without a drop of poetry in his soul or a thought in his head that hadn't been handed down for generations. His imagination ran only to the limits of the fences that bordered his father's fields that he would someday be heir to.

Soon enough, Goldilocks realized the purpose of his visit. The farmer's lad shook her father's hand and he in turn smiled and clapped him on the back. "Welcome to the family, my boy," her father said. "I'm sure she'll bear you many fine sons. Come, Goldilocks," he called. "Give your future husband a kiss on the cheek." And though her lips felt like lead and her heart ached to bursting, she did as her father asked.

"I beg your pardon," she said then. "May I please be excused? It's been a long, eventful day and I feel the need to rest." Goldilocks went into her bedroom and lay down on the quilt. After a moment, bitter tears filled her eyes and spilled out on the coverlet. A short time later, her mother stepped into the room, sat down beside her on the bed, and stroked her golden hair.

"Is he gone?" asked Goldilocks.

"Yes," her mother answered. "He will make you a good husband."

"Yes, Mama," said Goldilocks. "How much time do I have?"

"You are to be married at summer's end," she replied.

"But, Mama," she said, "I don't love him."

"You will learn to love him in time," her mother told her.

"Yes, Mama," Goldilocks answered; then she closed her eyes and fell asleep. Her mother sat for a time, biting her lip and telling herself it was all for the best. After a moment she got up and closed the door behind her.

That night, Goldilocks's disturbing dream returned, only this time, the face of the phantom husband belonged to the farmer lad. In her dream no matter how she yelled or cried out, again no one could hear her. She could touch no one, do nothing.

In a fury of frustration, she bolted from the house out into the approaching storm. She ran down the lawn, past the apple orchards and the formal garden, past the thicket of willow trees, to the pond where the white swans floated, heedless of the pelting rain.

Just as she reached the water's edge, a bolt of lightning rent the sky. In a great burst, the swans exploded into flight, filling the night with the beating of their mighty feathers and mournful clarion cries. As they circled higher and higher above her head, the white birds began to take on another shape and color. Their white plumage turned blacker than the night, their bodies pulled back into themselves, and when next the lightning lit up the darkness, Goldilocks could make out markings like cascading arcs of feathery violet and iridescent green along their wings . . . . And then she woke up.

It was the gray hour, just before the dawn. Goldilocks knew what she had to do. Noiselessly, she slipped out of her bed and tiptoed past her parents' room. By the door, she left a note that read simply, *I'm sorry your dreams can't be mine. I will always love you. Your daughter, Goldilocks.*

Some time later, she emerged from a clearing in the woods at the top of a hill. Below her, a log cabin sat, with smoke curling up from the chimney and a mailbox on the front lawn that read:

THREE
THE BEARS

Outside, Ox was chopping wood. When he saw her, he dropped his ax and they fell into one another's arms. Though they never married, and they fought on occasion, and it became necessary for them to build their own cabin a little further down the road to get away from the constant bickering of Mama's Bear and Rebound Bear, Goldilocks and Unorthodox Bear lived happily ever after — at least most of the time — which was good enough for them.

• • •

With all the pressure constantly being put on us to conform, the decision to buck the matrimony trend takes courage. It's hard to fight against the current when the message we're being sent — overtly or covertly — is that you can't be happy if you're not married. And sadly, though a lot of progress has been made, for many of us the social implications of being a single, strong, independent woman still seem to be mired in the past.

Treading the path of "singletude," whether for all time or just for the time being, isn't easy, but for some, not only is it a viable option, it's the only option. And once in a while, it's a choice we don't even realize we're making until we're well along a road we'd never dreamed we'd be traveling. And that's just what happened to Sophie.

"I can't remember a point in my life when I *didn't* want to get married," she relates. "I wanted the whole nine yards—the perfect mate, the big church ceremony, the white dress, bridesmaids, the formal reception . . . all of it. In fact, for a while there, I was so obsessed with the idea of finding a husband that it colored every decision I made. I'd be thinking things like, *I can't get a cat. What if I meet a man who's allergic? I can't stay home and be a couch potato on Saturday night, 'he' might be out there.* I'd make myself get up, put on my makeup, get dressed, and go out on the prowl. I went to singles dances and answered personal ads. And along the way, I met a lot of men, but no one I wound up marrying."

Eventually Sophie noticed a pattern in the men she was dating. They seemed to fall into one of two categories: they were either sweet guys she only wanted to be friends with, or interesting men she was drawn to have relationships with. Somewhere along the way she figured out that nice guys were a waste of time—for them and for her, because no matter how much she liked them, try as she might, she couldn't make herself love them. And sometimes she tried pretty hard.

"There would be times I'd think," admits Sophie, "that maybe I was just being too picky. Here was some really decent guy who wanted to have a relationship, even marry me, and I'd balk almost every time. I'd try to picture myself with him in five years, ten years, as an old couple, but I just couldn't do it." Sophie's logic boiled down to a simple equation: no spark, no chemistry, no go. So she stopped dating the Joe Normals who treated her nicely but didn't spark her passion. "It's funny," she admits, "I wanted all the same things that they wanted—just not with them."

After the "nice guys" came a series of men who stirred Sophie physically and emotionally, but totally lacked the commitment gene. "I had an on-again off-again relationship for almost ten years with a guy I was truly crazy about," she says, then adds with a laugh, "crazy being the operative word. I kept thinking at some point he was going to figure it out, tell me he loved me, and we'd get married. And finally, he *did* tell me he loved me and wanted to marry me . . . after I'd said enough is enough and I'd left him.

"Next came a great guy who is still one of my dearest friends. The only problem was when I met him, he was just getting separated from his wife and was totally down on marriage. Again, I thought that would change, but it didn't. So then came the guy who really loved me and wanted to marry me—and said so. Once we got to know each other better, we realized we were dead wrong for each other. But no hard feelings."

As she went from man to man, relationship to relationship, Sophie kept telling herself that she really wanted to get married, that she wanted the kids, the husband, and the house. But none of the men she was choosing turned out to be marriage material. As a matter of fact, they were cut from a different cloth altogether.

Says Sophie, "I'm not sure when it happened, but at some point, I began to doubt my own beliefs. There was a real battle raging inside me. One voice in my head was saying, *You like being on your own. You don't need a man to be satisfied with your life.* And, let me tell you, a major part of me didn't want to listen. It was like every time the one voice would pipe up, another was yelling, *Shut up! You're lying!* But it wouldn't shut up, and what I started to realize was that what I was hearing was the truth."

Time passed. Sophie wasn't unhappy. She was successful in her career and she found herself doing well enough to buy her own house, so she did. It wasn't a mansion, but it suited her. She decorated it the way she wanted to, and she found that she liked the fact that everything about it reflected some aspect of her personality. She didn't need to have someone else to make a home for her; she'd made her own, and that gave her a great—and wholly unexpected—sense of peace.

"Eventually it dawned on me, though I could scarcely believe it myself," she concedes, "that the reality was that I didn't really want to get married at all—or at least, I didn't *need* to. There were some components of marriage—the love, the sex, the intellectual challenge, being able to count on someone to be there for you and having someone be able to count on you, that I *did* want—but the rest of it didn't matter. You know that woman on the T-shirt who's slapping herself on the forehead, saying, 'Oops! I forgot to have kids!'? I'm like her. My life took a different path than the one I'd originally planned. But I'm okay with that."

As far as the future is concerned, Sophie is optimistic. "I don't know what's going to happen any more than the next person. I'm almost forty. I've been in a committed relationship for two years, but I don't see it leading to marriage. That might still happen someday, and it might not. Maybe I'll adopt kids, maybe I won't. I really love men and having them in my life, but I don't need to have one to make me whole. I don't think that makes me any less of a person. In fact, I know it doesn't. I'm living a good life, and to me that's what really counts."

Then there are women like Michelle, for whom the idea of marriage just doesn't hold water. "As far as I'm concerned," she confides, "the whole notion of 'plighting one's troth' and 'til death do us part' seems too drastic for me. Why should I jump through all the hoops and confound my life with red tape just to please some archaic convention in which I don't believe?"

Why indeed? Mostly because it's been drilled into us from so many sources that love doesn't count unless it's legal. But for Michelle, the ritual of marriage is more than a farce, it's downright hypocritical:

"I don't believe in making promises I can't, or don't, choose to keep," she contends. "As far as I'm concerned, so much of what marriage seems to be about has to do with interference by outsiders in what should be an entirely private matter. I don't want big brother, in the form of either the church or the state, regulating me as to whom or in what way I should love someone. I don't want them looking over my shoulder when I pay my taxes or fill out my insurance forms. I don't want them peering into my bedroom to make sure I'm not swinging from the chandelier or participating in a sexual act of which they do not approve. I don't want them to tell me I ought to go on living with someone I no longer love because that's what you're supposed to do. It's ludicrous."

Arden, a photojournalist in her late thirties, has already had, in her own words, "more lovers than I can count on my fingers and my toes," and sees no reason why she should change her course. "I'm not a particularly monogamous person by nature. Not that I would cheat on anyone I was with. Juggling lovers isn't my style. I just don't have a very long attention span. My record for a relationship is five years, but those were very unusual circumstances. It's usually two, and then I'm out.

"People tend to think of love as a finite thing," she continues, "but to me, that's dead wrong. I believe human beings have an infinite capacity for love, and I'm not sold on the concept that we have only one perfect soul mate out there for each of us. I want to keep exploring, to keep moving and growing. I want to fill my life with lots and lots of experiences and different shades of emotion. My taste in love is a lot like my taste in reading material: I adore collections of short stories, but I never have the patience for long novels. I always wind up having to flip to the last chapter to find out what happens at the end, and I'm usually disappointed."

Arden has made peace with the fact that she doesn't run with the crowd. She realizes that what she wants is different, but she doesn't see the need to waste her time trying to convince other people that her preferences are worthwhile. "Either they accept me or they don't," she says. "I don't like everyone, or expect that everyone will like me. I try to be tolerant of other people's choices, but how they live their lives is really none of my business, nor is my business theirs. I like being on my own too much to stay with one man forever, and also I don't particularly care for sharing my space with someone, even someone whom I love a great deal.

"I spend a great deal of my time at my photo studio. Between that and the traveling I do, I can be away from my home for weeks on end. I need to have a sanctuary, a place that's all mine, like an animal's den. It makes me feel trapped to know that when I get home, someone will be there. I much prefer staying in my lovers' apartments. That way, I have the luxury to come and go as I please."

Even if you are in the market for something long-term, there's no law that says you have to rule out a few little experiments with spontaneous combustion along the way. While you're waiting for Mr. Right, a fling with Mr. Right Now may be just what the doctor ordered. Not every love affair must lead to something permanent, and happily, sometimes the briefest candles burn with the brightest flames. Maybe you're not in a position to be in a committed relationship at the moment. Perhaps your job is taking you on a six-month assignment to a new part of the country, or, like Chloe, you've just ended a relationship and aren't looking to be tied down.

After a particularly long and nasty divorce, Chloe knew that she was not ready to take the plunge again, but after six months of staying home and feeling sorry for herself, she decided it was time to rejoin the living.

"I met Serge at the museum," she says. "He was standing in front of one of my favorite paintings, a Van Gogh . As I stood next to him, I could feel an energy, something electric, leaping between us. When he spoke, it was as if his voice had reached through my chest and grabbed my heart.

" 'Look at the brush strokes,' he said. 'So strong, so vivid . . . as if he had just painted them a moment ago and had stepped away into the next room to get something, as if at any moment he might return.'

"It was uncanny. He was describing the very thing I'd always felt when I looked at that painting. After about twenty minutes, we walked out of the museum hand in hand. We were talking about art and the strange force that flows through artists — genius, possession — whatever you'd call it, whatever it is that takes them over and demands to be expressed.

"We found ourselves back at my apartment. We walked up the three flights of stairs, still chatting away as if we'd known each other for a hundred years.

"We sat down on the couch and he began to caress me, and I him. We kissed, and it was that same feeling again—as if he'd reached in and taken hold of my heart. He kept telling me how beautiful I was, how precious. He made me feel appreciated, adored . . . alive.

"After we made love, he held me for over an hour," Chloe remembers fondly. "He sang little songs and stroked my hair. Every moment or two, he would lean over and kiss me, ever so gently . . . like the stroke of a brush.

"When he left, I knew I wasn't going to see him again. He was only in town for a few days and he was booked on a flight to Paris in the morning, but I didn't care.

"Of course, as I look back on the affair now, I'm surprised at myself, at how I behaved, but at the time, it seemed the most natural thing in the world. The afternoon I spent with Serge gave me back something I really needed. I felt healed. Beautiful. Blessed . . ."

Sophie, Arden, and Chloe each have valid reasons for not getting married. While all of them like men and incorporate them into their lives, they do it on their own terms. For them, the world does not revolve around being part of an authorized couple. These women feel neither desperate nor incomplete about the lifestyles they have chosen to pursue. They know that the power that controls their destinies belongs to them.

For Chloe (and women like her), marriage is an option, just not one she currently chooses to pursue. If somewhere down the road, she finds someone she feels comfortable enough with to embark on another long-term commitment, that will be up to her. But until such time as that happens, there's nothing wrong with her sampling the fruits from various orchards now and again—or even again and again.

Maybe you truly are one of those women who dream of finding their one and only someday, and if that's what you want, don't let anyone try to talk you out of it. Then again, maybe you're not monogamous by nature. Just because something was right for your sister, your mother, or even your best friend doesn't mean that it's right for you. After all, they aren't the ones who are going to have to live with the consequences; you are. And in the long run, if we're not happy with the choices we make, we've got no one to blame but ourselves.

Whatever you decide is right when it comes to the question of "to marry or not to marry"; you don't have to limit yourself by thinking that love only has one face or a single expression. There are as many variations to passion as there are freckles on a redhead. If your nature leads you away from the norm, don't sweat it, celebrate it. The path to joy has many roads. Take the one that pleases you. It's your best chance for getting where you really want to go.

CHAPTER 13

Down the Aisle... and What Comes After

SO WHAT'S THE DIFFERENCE between marrying and just living together? With today's nearly 50 percent divorce rate, some would argue, not much. However, a climate of "old-fashioned values" has begun to make a resurgence in this country, and as it continues to take hold, the flourishing wedding industry is pulling in record profits — proof positive that tons of men and women still want to "make it legal."

What does that say about us as a society? When something that has traditionally been looked on as a requirement — like marriage — is suddenly no longer mandatory, it generally becomes a luxury, and as such, is subject to the whims of fashion. In the counterculture sixties, many considered getting hitched bourgeois, passé, and even antilove. The "let it slide" seventies — a decade that will be best remembered for polyester and disco music — was an era when weddings were often considered too much fuss. Came the decade of the eighties, and along with it, the "Me Generation." So many young men and women were busy speeding along through life in the fast lane, they didn't bother to take time to settle down to share the wealth.

Now, fashion, being the pendulum it is, has swung back, and marriage is in style again, big-time. (Though, throughout that whole anti-marriage period, there were always those steadfast couples who continued to ride that middle wave and got themselves wed in spite of the popular current.) Should women worry that this back-to-the-future trajectory is going to force them to retreat into the unenlightened times when unmarried was unacceptable?

Thankfully, no, and that's because today's weddings are not "have tos," they're "want tos." For the most part, people who marry now aren't being forced by convention. Instead, they are electing to marry — to embrace a sense of community and celebrate a covenant — because that is their choice. Marriage still speaks to many couples with a voice that fills them with the prospect of joy and a feeling of belonging like nothing else in the human experience, and for those people there are many valid reasons to carry on the tradition.

Says Gwen, a twenty-eight-year-old teacher: "From the day Justin and I met, our love just grew and grew. It was right and we both knew it from the very beginning. After we'd been dating for a few months, marriage just seemed to be the next natural step in the progression — for both of us — so we began to make plans for the following summer.

"As things began to take shape, we realized we didn't have the budget for a huge reception or a fancy dress. We were going to have to cut some corners. I remember saying to Justin's mom that I didn't see how we were going to pull it off. But she just smiled and told me that things have a way of working themselves out.

"After our little talk, everything started to fall into place almost as if by magic. My aunt 'just happened to find' an antique wedding dress she'd forgotten about in her attic. It was really the loveliest thing I'd ever seen, and with a few alterations, it was perfect. The new bakery in town saw the announcement in the paper and phoned to say that since they were trying to drum up trade, they'd give us a big discount on the cake if we spread the word. All sorts of people—a flower arranger, a printer for the invitations—kept mysteriously finding their way to my door. These folks went to a lot of trouble to make our wedding happen. Of course, I've got Justin's mother to thank. She called my mom, and between the two of them, they set the ball in motion.

"Having our families, our friends, and the community chip in to help like that is what made the whole thing so special for us. It was like a gift we were receiving and a party we were giving all rolled up into one. It wasn't the most elaborate or expensive wedding, but it was beautiful all the same. The marriage was for us, but it was also bigger than just us, and that really made me feel connected to all of those wonderful people, and to God, as well."

Another woman who knew that someday matrimony would be the road she'd take was Althea, a thirty-nine-year-old office manager. "I waited a long time to get married," she confesses. "I sowed my wild oats, had my heart broken a few times. Got serious, then had to walk away. But when Eugene came into my life, I knew that what we had was somehow more than anything else I'd ever experienced before. I'd loved several men, some quite deeply, but no one I could ever picture saying 'now and forever' to, until him.

"The way I was raised, you never break a promise—if you can humanly help it—and marriage is the biggest promise of them all. Once you give your word, you don't just walk away when things get tough. It's like a binding contract, and that gives you an incentive to try harder, think more clearly, and see things through. The lesson I learned from my parents' marriage was that couples can learn to cope with things they thought they could never face, and come out stronger for it. And that's what I've always wanted for myself, and what I expect from the man who shares my life.

"Eugene and I have disagreements and arguments just like everyone else. But no matter how mad we get, that promise we made keeps us from losing perspective. It keeps us from crossing a line that too many couples cross without a second thought. It's taught me to be kinder and more patient, and even though I'm a fairly stubborn woman at times, it's also taught me to take a deep breath and look at things from the other side of the fence. And let me tell you, those are some valuable lessons."

One main reason that loads of men (and women) run screaming at the mere mention of the "M" word is that they cannot get their minds around the concept of being with only one person for the rest of their lives. They can't imagine waking up every morning next to the same face, making love to one body, till death do them part.

"Well, all I can say," relates Patrice, a happily married mother of two, "is that I feel sorry for those people. For love to reach a higher level, I believe you've got to make that commitment. Now I know that a lot of people have a problem with that. They see marriage as a limitation, but to me, it's exactly the opposite. As far as I'm concerned, love needs structure. Not to hold it back, but to set it free.

"When Josh and I fell in love, it was like two vines weaving together, reaching toward heaven with one common soul. If you give those vines direction and something to anchor themselves to, if you care for them and nurture them, they're going to thrive. If you don't do those things, love grows wild. Either it becomes a tangled mess that gets trampled under everyone's feet, or it strangles itself and everything around it. Sure, you can run off and plant a new vine somewhere else, but the same thing is bound to happen."

There are times in everyone's lives when being "child-like" is a fantastic thing. It opens our eyes to wonder, suspends our disbelief, and trashes our cynicism. It lets us be free to explore things that are new and untried. But there is a vast difference between being child*like* and child*ish*, and in marriage, it is a distinction that must be clearly made. As adults, we take actions and must accept the consequences for them. If others do not live up to our expectations at all times, it's up to us whether we're truly being deprived of something we need or are just acting out when we don't get our way.

In other words, you've got to take responsibility for your own expectations and not be too hasty to punish your mate if and when he can't fulfill them for you. It's all right to be angry, and it's all right to express feelings of hurt and disappointment, as long as you don't use your hurt and anger as weapons in an emotional war of one-upmanship.

"I have three brothers," explains Lori, "two older, one younger. We were always vying for our parents' attention, trying to be the 'good child.' If my brothers did something to make me mad, got me into trouble, or were given some special treat when I wasn't, I always had to get even. And it was pretty much the same with them. It was kind of like a game, but as we grew up, it became ingrained in our personalities.

"I didn't realize it at first, but this sibling behavior followed me into my adult relationships. Whenever one of my boyfriends did something I considered out of line, it was like he was throwing down a gauntlet.

"When George and I started dating, things went really well, until the first 'incident.' It was trivial. We'd showed up at a party a day late because George had misread the invitation. When we rang Greg's doorbell, he answered wearing a ripped-up T-shirt and cutoffs. There I was in my best dress, with a bottle of wine. Greg and George just laughed, but I was humiliated. Greg invited us in for some beer and pizza, but I was so furious, I stormed off and sat in the car.

"On the way home, I let George have it. We were due at his parents' house the following day, and I told him he could forget about it. It was at that point that he pulled the car over and said, 'Look, I know I made a mistake, and I'm sorry, but if this is the way you're going to behave, I don't think we should see each other any more. And it's too bad, because I really have strong feelings for you.'

"I was floored. Speechless. We spent the rest of the ride home in silence. When he pulled up in front of my house, I was still in shock. 'Look, Lori,' he told me, 'you can't treat people you care about this way and expect them to hang around. I screwed up, but not on purpose. I didn't do it to hurt you. You need to be able to let things like that go. Think about it.'

"And think about it I did. A lot. At first, I couldn't get past the anger. *Well, if that's the way he feels, good-bye and good riddance*, I told myself, but something kept nagging at me. And that something was the fact that deep down, I knew he was right. Now, I've never been one to apologize, and picking up that phone was the hardest thing I've ever done in my life. I must have dialed and hung up twenty times before I found the courage to let it ring.

"When he picked up the phone, my heart was in my mouth, but I managed to stammer out an apology. After that, we talked for nearly two hours. The relationship was back on again. We both knew that this issue wasn't going to just miraculously disappear just because we'd been able to put a name to it, but from that point on, things got a lot better, and whenever my old habits would rear their ugly heads, George would call me on it. And as angry as I might have been at those times, I'm glad he did. We've been married for four years now. I've finally learned that if you play at love like it's a game of one-on-one, you'll never win, but if you look at it as a team effort, nothing can beat you."

In our culture, many of us think about looking for our perfect soul mate as if it were a quest for the Holy Grail. But unfortunately, what happens to a lot of lucky lovers once they discover that incredible chalice of love and connectedness is that they simply heave a tremendous sigh of relief, then think to themselves, *Now that I've got it, I can bring it home, put it on the shelf, and it will take care of itself.* Wrong.

Says Corinne, who's taking her second ride on the marriage-go-round, "You can't just stop once that ring's on your finger. That was a mistake that both my first husband Harlan and I were guilty of, and in a way, I think that's what eventually eighty-sixed the marriage.

"We both came from backgrounds where getting married was very important to us. Family pressure, peer pressure, class pressure . . . all of it. But to me especially, getting married was the brass ring, and everything I did aimed me toward achieving that goal. The trouble was, I hadn't ever really figured out what was supposed to happen *after* you'd claimed your prize.

"I don't want to be too hard on Harlan, or myself for that matter. We were really young when we got married. I was seventeen, he was twenty. We were very impressionable. On the surface of things, I thought we made a perfect couple, and I think he felt the same. Once we got swept up in wedding fever, we never looked back until after we said our vows. We'd been so focused on getting to the altar, I guess we thought the next part would just come naturally . . . but it didn't.

"We'd never lived with anyone but our families before. We were used to doing things a certain way, and when that's not how it was anymore, we started to get mad at each other. The big problem was that we didn't know how to communicate. When he couldn't figure out what I wanted on his own, I began to resent him. When I wouldn't bend a little to let him have his way sometimes, he would resent me. The whole thing just kept going from bad to worse. It got to a point where it seemed like all we ever did was argue. Like I said, we were just kids really. By the time we figured out how bad it was, it was too late. We broke up a year later.

"After that relationship ended, I was really confused for a while, to say the least. Here I'd spent my whole life thinking that marriage was the be-all and end-all, and mine had turned out to be a major bust. I decided that I needed to go for counseling, and that is just what I did.

"Eventually, after some soul-searching and a heavy dose of common sense, I was able to figure out that it's not the wedding that counts, it's the marriage. Yes, that seems simple. But for me, it was one of those 'You can't see the forest for the trees' things. But let me tell you, when that revelation finally took hold, it changed me. First off, I was able to let go of a lot of the anger I'd felt toward Harlan and the disappointment I had with myself. We hadn't been bad people, just ignorant. Maybe we should have known better, but the truth was, we didn't. We hadn't meant to hurt each other, we just didn't have the tools or the know-how to stop it.

"Instead of looking for the next man I could marry right off the bat, I was determined to educate myself emotionally by dating some and playing the field. So, I took my time and taught myself to express my needs — in a nice way. I learned to be more open to compromise and less dependent on someone else to give me a sense of who I was. In short, I grew up. By the time Lloyd came along, I was finally ready, or at least I prayed I was.

"I thank God for every day this man is in my life, and now, hopefully, I've got the skills to make this marriage work. I try my best to keep the lines of communication open. I treat him the way I'd like to be treated, and I even let him have his way . . . *sometimes*. It isn't always easy. When we're tired, stressed out, what-have-you, some-times it's hard to make that extra effort, to put yourself in your partner's shoes, but you've got to keep at it. Believe me, it's worth it, too, because whatever you put in, you're going to get back, tenfold."

Finding the love of your life is not the end of the story, it's the beginning. Becoming part of a couple is not like reaching the finish line at the end of the race. Love is not a trophy, as I've said before—it's a living thing. All the groundwork you set up during courtship—honesty, open communication, flexibility, reasonable expectations, the Golden Rule, and so forth—can't just evaporate once you've hooked up with your Mr. Right. To ensure suc-cess, all of these elements, plus tolerance, patience, and a sense of humor, have to carry over to the next level. They are the foundation on which you build your spiritual home, the soil in which you plant the seeds of your future. Love takes work, but with the right spirit it will be work from which you derive satisfaction and enjoyment.

CHAPTER 14

A Walk in the Garden of Love

NOW, EVEN IN THE MOST perfect garden — or marriage — weeds will sprout, beetles and aphids may eat away at your bean plants, and storms will down your prize tomatoes from time to time. You're going to disagree. You're going to fight. It can't be helped. Into every human relationship some mischief will fall, but instead of spending time pointing fingers, laying blame, finding fault, or feeling guilty, try to uncover the underlying causes of your problems and correct them in the beginning.

• • •

Once upon a time there was a wealthy farmer who had four beautiful daughters, and as luck would have it, his neighbor to the east had four handsome sons of corresponding ages. As the children grew up, they were constantly in each other's company and in and out of each other's houses. Now, this being a story, and not the real world where lots of things go wrong, the children found themselves sorted out by natural pairs, fell in love, and decided to marry. That was the easy part.

The father of the brides was a generous man, whose fertile lands stretched out to the horizon. To each of his girls he made a gift of a hundred acres, a sturdy house, and all the furnishings they would require. The father of the grooms was a magnanimous man as well, and to each couple he made the gift of grain to plant, oxen to plow the fields, and all other equipment as was necessary to run a successful farm.

On the day of the wedding (for they all decided to marry at once) a great feast was planned, and all the neighbors from all the counties that lay close by—and from some that didn't—were invited. The guests began to arrive just after dawn, by cart and wagon, by horse and on foot. The farmyard soon began to fill with revelers and well-wishers of every description. Some brought gifts, according to their station, and others brought the good cheer and blessings that were all that they could afford. But rich or poor, all were made welcome.

At morning's end, the priest rode up on his mule, and seeing that the wedding party was assembled, he made ready to say the rites and hear the couples' vows before God. However, before he could begin, a strange thing happened. Just for a moment, a dark cloud passed across the sun, and a chill, bitter wind blew up a great cloud of dust in the road. Now, this was not magic, merely a trick of the weather, but the effect was very theatrical in any case, for when the wind had died down, the sun had returned, and the dust had settled, a stranger stood in the center of the gathering where no stranger had stood before.

This woman was dressed in a cloak as gray as ashes. Her face, though lined by age, was still fierce and beautiful. She turned to the father of the brides and said, "I have come far to bring your fair daughters a gift, John. Will you not greet me?" For a moment the farmer stood transfixed, as if suddenly turned to stone, his face ashen as the woman's cloak. "Well, John?"

With great effort, he broke himself from the spell of her gaze and stepped forward, his hand outstretched. "Miranda, it has been such a long time that I feared perhaps you were dead."

"Hoped, you mean?" she tossed back with a laugh that sent the chickens scurrying away in a panic.

"No, sister. You are most welcome here," he said humbly. At his words, a murmur ran through the crowd.

"And you, Jacob?" she demanded of the other farmer. "Are you glad that I have returned?" But the father of the grooms said nothing. To the assembled party, the woman then turned and spoke. "To you who do not know my tale, hear it now. When I was a girl, I loved this man Jacob with all my heart. He took my love and gave me his in return. We were to marry, but that never came to pass. A month before the ceremony, the man who owned the neighboring farm took ill. That farm is now Jacob's farm. He married the daughter of the landowner, and upon the man's death it became his.

"When I heard the news, I grew sick with despair. I begged my brother to avenge my grief. But he and Jacob were fast friends and shared many affairs of business. He told me to be reasonable, to try to see that what Jacob had done was for the best. My brother told me that I would always be looked after and taken care of, and since he is a man of his word, I know that would have been the case, but the bargain he asked me to accept did nothing to heal my wounded heart. Once I regained my strength, I left this place, vowing that someday, I would return. When I heard of the marriage of your children, I knew the time had come."

Then, smiling an odd smile, she pulled a basket from beneath her great cape. Inside the basket lay four white acorns, and next to them, three ornate ceramic pots, each one holding a different plant. The first had green, shiny tendrils that looked like jade in a waterfall; the second bore blossoms red as volcano fire; and the last, soft, furry leaves that gleamed like a pelt of sable in the moonlight.

Miranda stepped up to her nieces and offered them their choice. "Thank you, aunt," said each in turn, dropping her a curtsy as they made their selections. The eldest girl, who fancied herself more a lady than her sisters, chose the crimson flower because it was the most grand; the second, though she had desired the red blossom for herself, snatched up the green shrub; the third daughter, who had fancied the silvery plant anyhow, was pleased to make it her own. That left only the white acorns for the youngest sister, who, smiling, took one into her hand.

"My dear," said Miranda to this last niece, "by default, you have had no choice. If you prefer, I have other plants like the ones that I have given to your sisters. Give me back the acorn, and I will stop by your farm tomorrow."

"No, dear aunt, thank you very much all the same," the girl replied, shaking her head. "I think that if I plant the acorn and tend it well, someday a great tree may grow from it. And it would give me pleasure to try."

"And if nothing comes of it?" Miranda asked. "What will you do then?"

"I suppose I will dream of the tree that might have been, and take satisfaction in that."

"A wise answer, my child," said Miranda, stroking the girl's cheek. Then she picked up the remaining acorns and pressed them into the girl's hand, saying, "Plant only the one that you have chosen, but take the others for safe-keeping. You may find need of them later on," and with that, another cloud passed its hand over the sun. Soon enough, it departed, taking Miranda with it, and a few moments later, it was almost as if she had never been there at all.

The nuptial ceremony went on without further incident. And when the last ring was placed on the last finger and each of the brides had been soundly kissed, a great cheer went up amongst the company. Dance, song, food, and wine all flowed freely as the festivities—which lasted well into the night—ran their course. Finally, the revelers departed and the four brides and grooms retired to their separate farms and wedding beds to begin their new lives together.

That night, while the three elder sisters slumbered with contented smiles on their faces, the youngest found she could not sleep. Rising, she stood and walked to the open window, where she stood gazing out on the rolling land. Within a moment, her husband rose and came up behind her, and laying a gentle hand upon her shoulder, asked, "My darling, is something troubling you?"

She smiled up at his tender face and replied, "Perhaps you will think me silly, but I'd like to plant that acorn."

"Now?" he answered in disbelief.

"I suppose it could wait until morning," she replied, a small furrow creasing her brow.

"No," her husband replied gently. "Let it be as you wish." And the two of them walked out into the waning moonlight hand in hand and planted the seed at the end of the garden, taking care to water it well and mark the spot with a round, flat piece of slate. Then, giggling like children, they returned to their bed and fell asleep in each other's arms.

The next day, each of the other brides planted their aunt's wedding gifts in their own gardens as well. And in time, each began to grow, but as they did, curious circumstances began to occur. . . .

The eldest daughter's garden bloomed with a sea of flowers, red as blood. Their scent was intoxicating, and often in the morning, she would stroll through the grounds deeply inhaling the aroma. After a time, she found that when her husband would return from his day's work, his countenance filled her with disgust. No matter what he did, it was never good enough. Eventually, she came to think that he existed merely to annoy her. She spent her days planning how to rid herself of him, her nights in icy, furious silence. For what the girl did not know was that the thing her aunt had given her to plant was anger, and as it thrived, her love and happiness waned, until even their memory seemed some sort of sad joke. After three weeks, the husband moved out to the barn, and when they passed one another, they could not find a civil word to say, so they said nothing.

Now, the second daughter had planted jealousy in her garden, and as it multiplied, she became more and more consumed by envy and the want of things that were not rightly hers. The thick vines spread and tangled, swallowing up everything in their path. She began to carp and whine about this thing she did not have and that, and she started to suspect the truth of her good husband's love for her. Their life became a hell on earth filled with spiteful allegations and mistrust. No matter how strongly the husband protested, she would have no part of his explanations or assurances. One night, less than a month later, he went off to the town and would not come home.

As the third daughter's plant grew, it seemed harmless enough and very beautiful. Spreading quickly, it soon covered the garden with its pewter mantle. At first, the girl would rise each day, look out her bedroom window, and note the plant's progress. Then, she would dress and begin her chores. But one morning, a strange mood overtook her as she gazed across her garden. Instead of bathing and putting on her clothes, she pulled a rocking chair up to the windowsill and sat down.

When her husband arrived home that evening, she was still there, her chores undone and supper never started. Concerned, the good lad sat down next to her to see what was the matter, but the moment he joined his wife, he too was transfixed by the plant's hypnotic spell.

A week passed, then another, then a third. The two worried fathers, not having heard from their children, jumped into a wagon and sped hastily to their farm. When they arrived, their eyes were met with a truly bizarre sight: the silvery plant had engulfed the entire garden and the farmhouse in a thick coat of dreamy gray.

With much effort, the two fathers pulled the front door asunder, calling to their children to come out and make themselves known, but there was no answer. What they discovered in the bedroom nearly broke their hearts, for there by the window sat the young couple sheathed from head to toe in a cocoon of cottony floss. Frantically, the two old men pulled the stuff from their unmoving faces, and though they were not dead, they neither stirred nor spoke, for the plant that grew in their garden was apathy, and for all the efforts the old men made, they were unable to reverse its course.

Despairing, the two men climbed back onto the wagon. Fearing the worst, they went to see how their other children were faring, and in each case they were met by calamity—until, that is, they reached the farm of the youngest couple, where all appeared to be well. The husband was out in the fields, tending his crops, but the wife met them at the door, looking cheerful and content. Alarmed at the old farmers' appearance, she hurried them into the kitchen, sat them down by the hearth, and made each of them a cup of tea. "Now, tell me what has happened," she urged the men. "What has brought you to such grief?"

So the two men, shaking with tears of sorrow, detailed the tragic turns that had befallen her sisters and brothers-in-law. The girl listened very carefully, then said, "Fathers, you must fetch my husband and any strong young men from the village who will assist us, for I know what must be done. Bring hoes and rakes, axes and shovels. Bring dry wood, kindling, and a strong cart. We must depart at once for the farms of my sisters and their husbands. I only pray we are not too late."

The old men did as the young wife bid them. They gathered such men as they could find along with the things she had asked for and assembled at the oldest sister's farm. "To the garden," the young wife said, "and tear up every root and leaf and flower of that red-blossomed plant and put them in the cart."

Her eldest sister screamed curses at her and ran from the house like a hellcat bent on destruction, but the youngest sister charged the men to hold her back. Finally, after some time, when every trace of those flowers of destruction had been rent from the ground, the youngest sister reached into her pocket for one of the three remaining white acorns and planted it in the ground. Almost immediately, a seedling sprouted from the earth, and as it did, the elder sister's anger fell away. In but a few moments, she was back to her former self. Her husband came out of the barn and took her gently in his arms. She wept tears of apology; then they joined the others, and together the group made its way to the farm of the next sister.

Now, the vines of jealousy were thick and tenacious. It took the men the better part of the afternoon to wrest them from their hold on the garden, but finally, some hours later, exhausted by their efforts, they threw the last of the malicious mess onto the cart to join the remains of the red flowers. Again, the youngest wife took from her pocket a white acorn and planted it in her sister's garden, and no sooner had the dirt closed over it, than it sprouted.

"What have I done?" the second sister cried. "I have driven away the only man I've ever loved, and he would be well within his rights never to speak to me again." But her husband, who had heard the commotion in town and come to see what the fuss was about, stepped forward.

"We have been in the hold of some dark magic," he said, "but that night has passed, and we shall speak of it no more."

By the time the company reached the third sister's farm, the sun had nearly set. The eerie silence of the place chilled them to the bone. But the youngest daughter told them that there was no time to waste. They set to work tearing up the silver growth that blanketed the farmhouse, and finally, with the moon looking down from his chariot in the sky, their labor was complete. Taking the last acorn from her pocket, the youngest wife proceeded to plant it in the garden. For a moment, to everyone's horror, nothing happened. Then, slowly, a bud began to emerge, and as it sprouted, the sleeping sister and her husband awoke with wonder.

"We have two last tasks to accomplish before sunrise," the youngest wife said. Leading them to the cart that held the remains of all the spiteful weeds her sisters had mistakenly planted, she said, "This must be destroyed, so that no foul seeds of their ilk shall ever sprout again." And with that, the men pulled the cart out into a fallow field, took the kindling and the wood, and burnt up the evil crop they had harvested that night.

"Now all is done," said the girl's father. "Rightness has been restored."

"Yes," agreed Jacob. "It is finished. Let us put the past behind us and move on."

"No," said the youngest daughter. "It is not finished. For as you say, we must put the past behind us, but not until we have learned the lessons it has sought to teach us."

"Daughter," farmer John asked, "what do you mean by this speech?"

"The thing which your sister offered all of us to plant in our gardens was true love, but my sisters chose instead to sow the seeds of anger, jealousy, and apathy, and you see what destruction it brought them."

"Your aunt is an evil woman," the girl's father began to protest, "she had no right . . ."

But the young girl cut him off. "When true love is taken lightly or thrown away," she said, "how can you expect any other outcome?" Then she turned to Jacob and continued: "By denying your love for her and hers for you, you set that woman on a hard, lonely road. Love will find a home if you let it and will create despair if you will not. This is an evil that you sent forth yourselves. You can't make up for the damage you have caused, but now acknowledge your part in this sadness, and apologize."

"But Miranda is not here," Jacob protested.

"She will hear you, anyway," said the girl. "I'm sure of it."

So, the two men, hats in hand, looked toward the east and the rising sun, and each of them tearfully accepted blame for his part in Miranda's fate and begged that she forgive him.

From that day on, all of the couples flourished, and on each of their farms a tree of true love grew. Though from time to time, a red flower would sprout in the oldest daughter's yard, the next oldest would find a green tendril poking its sly head out from beneath the garden soil, and the third girl would spy a hint of gray lichen clinging to the arbor — for such things once planted can never be got rid of altogether. So, for the rest of their lives, the girls and their husbands had to be vigilant. And when a mood of anger, jealousy, or apathy came on them, they would immediately go to their gardens, seek out the offending weed, and pull it up by the root.

As for the youngest girl and her husband, their tree grew straight and tall and strong. For some people, the lucky ones, know a good thing when they hold it in their hand.

• • •

Happy Endings

In his groundbreaking book *The Art of Loving*, Dr. Erich Fromm talks about a trap into which human beings too hungry in their search for the perfect soul mate often fall. He equates our overwhelming desire to know what makes love work and how we can keep it forever to ripping the wings off a butterfly to see what makes it fly. You can dissect the anatomy, but in so doing, you destroy the miracle. So, if you're searching for some secret formula that will wrap love up and put it in your pocket, forget it. The answer to this question is multiple choice.

Love, like any living thing, is something we can never truly own, and no rules that we apply can ever hope to circumscribe it. The soul of love, like that of a lion, does not thrive caged inside a zoo; no matter how humane the keeper, or how well-kept the confines, the wild heart within never forgets its yearning to be free. You'll be much better off living the magic than questioning where it comes from or trying to bottle it for mass consumption. Just remember a couple of basic things, and you'll be fine:

- **What's Sauce for the Goose Is Sauce for the Gander:** Love is a fifty-fifty partnership. Your lover's needs are important, but no more so than yours. There is no dishonor in compromise, as long as it's a two-way street. But if you're the one making all the sacrifices, just get off the bus and wait for a better one to come along.

- **Without You, I'm Something:** As any of you know if you've read *Pygmalion* or seen *My Fair Lady*, the hero, Professor Henry Higgins, doesn't fall for the heroine, Eliza Doolittle, until she steps out from under his thumb and storms off on her own. In one crystallizing, cathartic moment, they both realize that she is truly his equal, "a consort battleship," as he puts it. And it is only then that he wants her.

  Of course, by that point, as well she should, she tells the overbearing, unappreciative blowhard to take a hike (and in the book, she doesn't run back to him so the audience can have its happy ending, either. She marries Freddy . . . arguably not the best choice, but at least it's hers and not some studio exec's out to boost ticket sales). She has a life, and she is free to do with it as she likes and dispense her love as she pleases. And most important, she is still herself. She has become what my Grampa Max used to fondly call "a broad."

Ah, to be a broad in the next millennium. . . . I know, I know. Broad is no longer a PC term — but to me it evokes the image of those great, tough women who gave as good as they got — and better. Women with nicknames like Toots and Babe, who were responsible for their own fates; whose days were filled with adventure and whose nights were colored by passion. In the movies, I didn't find my idols in the glamour of Garbo, the humor and ultimate tragedy of Monroe, or the hard-edged sophistication of Bette or Joan.

Me? I wanted to be Jean Arthur. Remember her? Lovely, but not really beautiful; smart, quirky, funny, indomitable, ever wise, always real — with enough heart to save the soul of any man and not lose herself in doing it. That was my kind of broad, and if that's the kind of broad that some of you end up being, then the next millennium may be the best one of all.

If you're not part of a happy couple yet, and it's driving you crazy, quit worrying that love isn't ever going to knock on your door. Water has a way of finding its own level. Once you remove the obstacles that you yourself have put up, love will figure out what route it needs to take to get to you. Take a deep breath. Give it time. Go to the movies. Love may be waiting for you on the front porch when you get home.